DONE WITH BROKE

Latifat Akintade, MD

Done
WITH
Broke

**The Woman Physician's Guide
to More Money and
Less Hustle**

LIONCREST
PUBLISHING

DONE WITH BROKE
The Woman Physician's Guide to More Money and Less Hustle

FIRST EDITION

ISBN   978-1-5445-4112-9 *Hardcover*
       978-1-5445-4111-2 *Paperback*
       978-1-5445-4113-6 *Ebook*
       978-1-5445-4114-3 *Audiobook*

To every woman who has tolerated less pay, less money. This is dedicated to you. To liberate you. To empower you and to hear you roar!

You are worthy. You are born to be wealthy.

Contents

Introduction

Let me tell you about Susan.

Susan is an internal medicine physician in her forties. She became a doctor because of her desire to serve; growing up, service was part of how you made a difference. She was raised in a middle-income family who prioritized working hard. Her parents always told her, "If you want to succeed, you have to work hard." But beyond her parents telling her to work hard, she doesn't remember having conversations about money at the dinner table. Now, with a family of her own including three children, she finds herself struggling to balance her time—and her checkbook.

Susan sees a lot of pain and stress in the medical workplace. Sometimes she works eighty hours a week or is called at two o'clock in the morning to take care of an emergency. There are days when she wishes she could just take a break. Working so many hours feels unsustainable. She's worried about burnout. She would like to cut down to working four days a week. The main factor stopping her is money. Yes, the M-word. She's carrying multiple six figures of student-loan debt. With her long hours, she feels guilty for not spending as much time as she'd like with her kids, so she pays for them to have the best of everything. Her parents are pressuring her to support them as they reach retirement age. Thankfully, her paycheck comes in every two weeks so she doesn't have to worry quite yet. Her bills and student loans will be taken care of. But she's not growing her wealth.

It's hard for her to talk about her problems because how does she tell someone that she doesn't know much about money? She's tried looking up information in the past, but what she finds looks like a different language from a different planet.

She wants to learn how to manage her finances better, privately, and safely; she wants a roadmap but doesn't know where to seek it out. She knows if she could learn how to think differently about her money, things would change.

She wants to be a physician and a good mom with financial security.

She wants to have money and trust that she can have it, grow it, and use it. She knows that in order to have what she wants, she has to learn and make changes. She can't keep doing the same thing and expect a different result. She knows that she has to start.

Does that sound familiar?

Susan is a fictional character. She represents the stories of hundreds of thousands of women physicians. I was one of them too. I thought getting paid six figures was going to mean automatic wealth or at least comfort. But wealth didn't come automatically because no one taught me how to manage my money.

At the start of my attendingship, I decided I was going to accept an employed position in academia or a large multispecialist group. I knew this path would probably put me on a one-way trip to being burned out and disempowered. After all, during my residency, I had witnessed my attendings becoming burned out by a system in which physician autonomy was increasingly lost. But with the debt I was carrying, I didn't feel like I had a choice. My net worth was very negative and having a sense of secured income was very attractive.

When the income came, I didn't quite know what to do with it. So instead of telling it what to do, I let it do what it wanted. Interestingly, my income did grow, but my net worth wasn't automatically increasing. It didn't feel like I thought multiple six-figure income was going to feel like. For most people, that may sound strange. But for physicians with multiple six figures in student debt, plus childcare, and extended family financial responsibilities, it doesn't take a lot for that post-tax income to vape away. It felt like the money was leaking out of my control.

I was ready to feel successful.

I started on my money journey to solve my own money problems and lack of financial literacy. I quickly found out that most of the money spaces were not made with me in mind. In order to go from broke to having money, I had to unlearn many things. I had to reset my money mindset from a poverty mindset to a wealth mindset. It was a messy process of learning. As I worked on solving my own money issues, I began to realize that I was not a unicorn.

MONEY IS SIMPLE

As doctors, we are smart, amazing, badass women who spend days solving complicated problems. Money does not have to be a complicated problem; the biggest hurdle is reframing our mindset. After that, the rest is simple.

Medical training did an excellent job of teaching us clinical skills and puts us in the position to earn an income that is well above the average national income. However, we were not taught how to understand this income or how to see it as a seed that can grow into a tree. This has led to physicians living paycheck to paycheck or being easy targets from the shiny-suited, kind-appearing salespeople that masquerade as financial advisors.

I was actually surprised that once I got over my own brain drama, money wasn't complicated. It was easier than most classes I took in undergraduate and medical school. My only wish was that I had learned this earlier. I could have traded another Kreb cycle memorization class for something as important and impactful as this.

My own money journey eventually led me to share the tips that I learned with other women physicians. After coaching hundreds of women physicians, I started seeing patterns that would eventually lead to wealth building. I began to see the key pillars that eventually became the core curriculum that I now teach female physicians. I may not be a finance expert, but I have found the tools that worked for me and other women physicians to get control of our finances.

First, you change your mentality toward money and the various aspects of wealth. You learn to follow your money to see where it is going. This includes both your spending and investments. Then you learn the basic foundational language of the stock market. If you can memorize so many biochemical pathways, pharmacology, and mechanisms of diseases, you can learn the language of money. Finally, you learn to diversify your investments in a way that is in line with your values, lifestyle, and goals. That's it!

Just like the CEO of a company doesn't do every single thing herself, the same goes for money. However, when you are equipped with the core knowledge, you will be best suited to build, screen, and lead your team under your directorship as the badass woman that you are.

In Chapter 1, you will learn how we got here. The culture of medicine and the systems of oppression have negatively impacted the world of money for women. When you understand and see it, it's impossible to unsee it. That's a good thing. Let it infuriate you. Let it lead to self-awareness and then let's fix it. We are done banging our head against the wall in frustration; just like when a car bumps into a wall, it doesn't keep driving into the wall. Instead, you disengage, reframe, and then reengage in a different direction or intensity.

In Chapter 2, we will explore how your upbringing and family experiences impact your finances. We will explore both the intentional learning and the subconscious programming, all of which creates the foundation on which the rest of your money experiences lie. For immigrants and women who grew up in low socioeconomic households, seeing the ongoing effects of racism and sexism and how it relates to wealth, all these factors will work together to determine our financial stories: how we are who we are today, how we think about wealth, how to spend, save, and have. All of it. It is essential to pick what's serving your future and ditch the rest. First, you have to unlearn, then learn.

It is also critical to understand this is not the space for guilt or shame. Those are completely part of the normal human experiences but some of the least useful emotions. Blaming or faulting your parents or guardians isn't a productive use of energy or time. They did what they did. We get to choose how we pivot next. If we don't change, the future generations will have questions for us too.

In Chapter 3, we will explore your relationship with money as a key component of your relationship with self. How we treat money is a reflection of how we treat ourselves. My concept is simple: transform one and transform the other. The wealth you want to create is the result of a transformed relationship with self.

In Chapter 4, we will walk through rethinking spending. Many of us spend in a way that is not intentional. We have been taught that cutting spending is how you build wealth. This may have served some people. However, it can lead to hoarding and low rates of investing because spending makes us nervous. If we can revolutionize how we think about spending, we as women will learn to love how we spend, we will buy more assets, we will focus on the real wealth-growing activities of investing—and our net worth will increase as a result.

In Chapter 5, we will explore the importance of changing the prevalent mentality toward debt. You can avoid debt and still build wealth. However, historically, women and people of color have had less access to income-generating debt and the knowledge of how to leverage it. This knowledge is essential to closing the wealth gap and building that wealth mindset. Also, as physicians, we tend to have student loan debt. We don't have to hate it to pay it off. You can choose a more neutral emotion; it will improve your life's experience without negatively impacting your pay-off plans.

In Chapter 6, we will discuss why it is essential that we spend at least the same amount of energy thinking of investment as we spend on thinking about spending. Investments are where real wealth is found. Saving alone isn't how we build wealth. Investing is how we build wealth. We will also explore some misconceptions and myths surrounding investments. Changing the financial future of women physicians will require shifting our focus. Simple investments win!

In Chapter 7, you will learn how the culture of side hustle can contribute toward fatigue and exhaustion. If you think of your business as a side hustle, you will earn a side hustle kind of income. If you think of each business as its own full entity, you will create systems and you will build and grow. It is also important to mix and match active and passive income.

As women physicians, we are more likely to lead with heart. That's a good thing. Our perceived morality surrounding money and wealth is important in determining whether we grow toward wealth or we consciously or subconsciously grow away from it. In the words of my friend Dr. Una of EntreMD Business School, "Money is paper with dead people's faces on it." Money is like water. It has no shape. It takes the shape of its container. You are the container. You decide the morality. I believe women are key players in determining the future of wealth. We already know what the world looks like when we control a minority of the wealth. Let's see what happens as we close that gap. It's an experiment I'm willing to bet on. We will cover the gap in Chapter 8.

In Chapters 9 and 10, we will discuss how we build the new generational wealth, how we can change family trees, and how we curate our own rich lives in a way that's in line with what we want to see in the world.

THE UNDERDOG ADVANTAGE

The gender and racial bias in medicine is strong. We need more women at the table who are financially confident and free to speak and advocate without fear of retaliation. We need to harness the power of our own underdog advantage.

The idea of underdog advantage relies on the concept of turning your "disadvantage" into an advantage. You may argue that physicians are not underdogs, but when it comes to money, we are. The reason why we let ourselves be mistreated by admin and insurance companies is exactly because we are not owning our complete power.

In his book *The Underdog Advantage*, Dean Graziosi discussed key points that were essential in helping him succeed despite his underdog position. First, underdogs turn desperation into persuasion. Second, underdogs are relentlessly resourceful.

Are we willing to turn our desperation into persuasion? Sometimes, that persuasion is to ourselves. Other times, it is to negotiate our incomes or negotiate with investors, partners, or other teams we put together as part of buying our own wealth stories.

As physicians and also as women, there is no one more prepped in the art of resourcefulness. When a patient comes to the clinic or the hospital and we can't tell exactly what's going on, we lean into resourcefulness. We order blood tests, imaging studies, we consult colleagues, or talk to our own colleagues. When all that fails and we still cannot figure out what ails our patient, we dig into the literature, get up to date on the most recent findings, look for case studies, and find other experts at other centers if needed.

Don't ever believe the lie that you are not resourceful. We simply do it so automatically and so routinely that we have stopped seeing how uncommon this is. It took years of training from medical school to fellowship to own this. Now you simply have to direct your resourcefulness into areas that will bring you more money and, ultimately, more freedom of time.

When physicians are not afraid to walk, things will change. When we are not relying on our clinical income only and trust our ability to pivot it and create options financially, things will change.

TIME TO ACTIVATE OUR MONEY BRAINS

I believe we all have wealthy brains. During a recent conversation, I told a friend that making money moves is like playing chess. You look at the players you have and decide where to move. The ability to move your money, tell it where to go, and analyze the risk and benefits of your decision in a way that is unique to you is the core feature of a wealthy brain.

For a long time, my brain was dormant. I honestly thought money was all just math. It also didn't quite make sense either because I have excelled in calculus and, like many physicians, I excelled in complex topics. But I didn't know that being money savvy required a kind of critical thinking skill I hadn't been taught yet. The beautiful thing is, within a short amount of time, I have been able to rewire my own money brain. Subsequently, I created a lot of amazing money wins in the process. If I can do it, of course you can too.

Just as I had learned to use my clinical brain for patient care, I can now use my money brain to master and build on the same foundations you will learn in this book. I went from broke to millionaire in about five years without investing in individual stocks, without a complicated pathway, without selling my soul to the devil, and without working extra shifts. Within three years since my initial come-to-Jesus moment, I paid off about $200,000 in debt and achieved financial liberation through investing in index funds, real estate, and business. I have distilled the information into a framework that you will learn. At the end of this book, you will have the key essential toolkit that will help you change your money brain.

Here is the truth.

You can learn how to have money, use it, spend it, and build it.

You can own your money brain.

First, you have to unlearn some of the nonsense we have been taught and build a more optimal foundation.

Are you ready to learn the foundation that will help you build your money brain so you can create your definition of a rich life?

Let's go!

CHAPTER 1

I Have Arrived

When I moved to the United States at the age of eighteen, my goal was to become a doctor. I had seen how medicine was practiced growing up and seen the impact that physicians played in the lives of so many people. I wanted to help people be well and feel better. I didn't know how, but I had a mission: to be a good physician who cared for humans. The road here was filled with a lot of late-night coffee, thirty-hour ICU shifts in my third trimester of pregnancy, and many years of delayed gratification.

So when I finally graduated fellowship, I thought I had finally made it! I am now a gastroenterologist. Years and years of training has finally paid off. I am ready for that paycheck that I had dreamed of for many, many years. Now I can finally pay off that student loan, buy that house I have always wanted, and give back.

Do you remember that moment for you? Graduating fellowship or residency. That relief! Finally done. Now, you thought, you would be able to help people live their best, healthiest lives. You would be able to buy your dream house and pay off your debt and not worry about money at the end of every month.

Unfortunately, most of us are not given the tools to practice medicine on our terms. We are not given the tools to be free from worry about money. This leads to both internal and external stressors that impact our financial well-being.

In a publication in *Quartz* in 2018, Melinda Gates stated that when money flows into the hands of women, everything changes.[1] If we want to change the culture of unwellness in medicine, we have to get money in the hands of women. Burnout would decrease because we would grind less and have choices in how we spend our time and lives. We would be more free to use our creative brains and time to serve in even bigger ways within and outside the hospital walls.

Mastering the content discussed in this book is essential in freeing your minds, in your journey to money, your journey to existing with money, and unlocking your own true financial freedom.

Now let's dive in.

TALKING ABOUT MONEY

Kate is a woman physician. She had been in practice for about three years when a new male physician joined her practice. During a leisurely conversation, she found out he was earning a solid $70,000 per year more than she was. She was shocked. She

---

1   Melinda Gates, "Melinda Gates: When Money Flows into the Hands of
    Women, Everything Changes," Quartz, March 5, 2018, https://qz.com/1220879/
    melinda-gates-when-money-flows-into-the-hands-of-women-everything-changes.

thought she had been offered a good income. After all, she was earning more than she had ever earned or more than anyone in her family had ever earned. She also assumed other humans in medicine were held to a high code of conduct. She had trusted and hoped the offer she was given was fair.

They walked over to their HR department. You know why they said there was a disparity? She was told it was because she did not ask. What the heck?

Money remains a taboo topic in medicine.

When money conversations are taboo, we don't have them easily which affects our net worth. A lack of fluency and the secrecy around money has contributed to our reputation of being poor negotiators.

In an ideal world, our negotiating skills wouldn't matter, but the world isn't ideal. Keeping our silence about money affects us. Unless we are ready to change the culture of silence around money, we will continue to struggle and be paid inequitably.

This silence around money especially affects female physicians. Women in medicine in general earn less than their male counterparts. Recent published data has shown that over the lifetime of our career, women physicians will make about $2 million less than our male counterparts.[2] Women earn less than men in more

---

2   Morgan Smith, "Women Earn $2 Million Less than Men as Doctors over a 40-Year Career, according to a New Study," CNBC, December 20, 2021, https://www.cnbc. com/2021/12/20/study-women-earn-2-million-dollars-less-than-men-as-doctors-over-their-career.html#:~:text=Work-,Women%20earn%20%242%20million%20less%20than%20 men%20as%20doctors%20over,according%20to%20a%20new%20study&text=Female%20 doctors%20are%20paid%20significantly,The%20study%2C%20published%20Dec.

than 90 percent of academic medical specialties. This discrepancy holds true at both the start of their careers and ten years later. Some of these differences may show up as varied rates of sign-on bonuses offered. We also know that women of color, specifically Latinas and African Americans, are at the bottom of the earning pole.[3] In fact, specialties that are more concentrated by women tend to earn less.[4] It is a common saying that where the women flow will show you where money isn't.

As female physicians, we also suffer from selective volunteerism. We are more likely to be volunteered for nonpaying roles—for example,. one more committee. We are expected to participate after hours without compensation. When we decline, we are called non-team players. What the heck? Are you pissed yet? I know I was and continue to be when I'm reminded of how ridiculous that is.

We are changing that narrative. Imagine a world where women are paid based on their expertise and the value added and not due to the subconscious bias that exists in medicine today. Picture a world where our clinical income becomes one of our many sources and every physician has the framework that will take us to multiple six and seven figures, so we can have the choice to live on our terms. That new reality is why I am excited that you are reading this. It means time is up.

3   Stephanie Hedt, "New Study Finds Pay Gaps in Physician Income by Race, Gender," press release, USC Schaeffer, June 15, 2016, https://healthpolicy.usc.edu/article/new-study-finds-pay-gaps-in-physician-income-by-race-gender/.

4   Victoria Forster, "Gender Pay Gap Affects Most Medical Specialties, Persists over Time," Cancer Therapy Advisor, April 22, 2022, https://www.cancertherapyadvisor.com/home/general-medicine/gender-pay-gap-medicine-persists-across-specialties-over-time/.

THE COST OF PRACTICING MEDICINE

Sarah is a divorced mother of three children. Her three children are age six and under. Because of her busy, sometimes sporadic hours, having reliable childcare is an essential need as she provides care to her patients at all hours of the day and night. She had been able to find a reasonably priced day care center that came highly recommended by some of her neighbors. She hired additional help with drop-off and pickup before and after day care. When she is on call, she pays a higher nighttime rate to provide safe childcare for her children.

Thinking about the cost of childcare is a big source of stress for her. On the one hand, she is grateful she has been able to find amazing, safe members of her childcare team whom she trusts. However, she feels the stress and burden of paying such a significant percentage of her post-tax income for childcare. She wishes she could save for their future college funds and feels some guilt about not having any money saved for that purpose.

She is also very grateful for modern-day resources like grocery delivery and Amazon delivery. However, those sometimes come at a higher price point than going to the store herself.

Sarah is very stressed out. She recently agreed to meet up with some local friends on a Saturday night. After getting bombarded with questions about how to deal with hemorrhoids, she decided it wasn't the stress relief she was hoping for. She paid for her drinks, went home, laid in her bed, and mentally prepped herself to not let her stress and emotions show on her face.

Sarah's finances are a huge source of stress for her. At the end of the month, she finds herself holding her breath and praying nothing happens to her next paycheck.

Her finances are far from what she hoped they would be when she decided to be a physician. She loves her kids dearly. She loves her patients dearly. She wishes she could just get a financial break!

Like Sarah, burnout wasn't included in my plan for success. I didn't know that there were so many physicians experiencing moral injury in medicine—and this was before the COVID pandemic that started in 2019.

It is interesting how the public talks about physician income, but no one talks about the cost of practicing medicine at odd hours. As physicians working long shifts, there is an associated cost of childcare or adult care so that you can get to the hospital even in the middle of the night. The cost of the emotional spending that comes along after working your thirtieth hour straight or after going weeks without seeing loved ones. When you have less free time, you are more likely to shop for convenience, which may be associated with higher cost.

If you are a woman of color, the deck may be further stacked against you. We know you are more likely to be volunteered for roles that are not financially compensated. You are more likely to receive plaques and verbal thank-yous for your contributions. However, when it comes to financial compensation, you will likely be found at the bottom.

As physicians, our stress is made worse by our increasing lack of job security. Like many physicians, I thought my income was always going to be guaranteed. I am a freaking physician. Everyone is always going to need a physician, right? I never imagined I would live in a day when physicians are fired for no reason. This was not an uncommon story, especially during the COVID-19 pandemic. Being an excellent clinician isn't even protective. It seemed like fitting in a box was more valued than actually providing excellent care.

Most of us were taught you practice medicine until we are old and gray. You know, the whole "medicine is a calling" thing. Don't get me wrong, I still believe it is. In fact, I love clinical medicine. However, how we were taught in the past was a sacrificial lamb, forget yourself, ignore yourself kind of way. We believed we could work anywhere in the world. Yes, you may need to get certified to work in that local place, but ultimately, your degree guarantees you an income-producing job.

That is what we have been sold. It is what we have been made to believe.

Being a physician is still a calling, but with the experience of physician colleagues across the country, diminished insurance reimbursement, and the effect of practicing medicine in a Google-doctor world, it's no surprise physicians are getting progressively tired.

Let's talk about the doctor tax for a second (not the IRS one, although that's a big component). Doctor tax refers to the inflation in prices typically for services or goods when people find out you are a physician. Many physicians groups and conversations are full of examples of these "doctor taxes." It's no wonder many physicians hide their occupation outside of work. That and the fact that having random humans talk to you about hemorrhoids and abdominal pain at cocktails isn't the idea you had in mind when you decided to attend that cocktail event.

The bottom line is whether you are employed or own your own

practice, it is clear that the internal and external financial stressors don't help.

THE DICHOTOMY BETWEEN I HAVE ENOUGH VERSUS I DON'T HAVE ENOUGH

As a fellow graduating fellowship, I couldn't find communities or spaces where I could discuss the unique challenges that women faced financially. Nothing. Many of the communities were filled with "splaining and shaming." We carry enough shame of our own that needs to be released. You are shamed for having, shamed for not having, shamed for not knowing. It's like we are groomed to find solace and peace in average.

When conversations come up about money, one half of the room says we should be grateful because at least we earn an income.

When did barely become enough? We can't talk about enough without mentioning our individual capacity to have money.

Our capacity when it comes to money is our ability to have, expansively in a way that is wealthy minded. We all have varying capacities to have. This is the potential for growth that can exist without grinding or hustling. This is similar to our capacity to eat or the amount needed for satiety. It varies per individual. How, then, can we define enough?

First, you need to know your minimum viable expense. This term refers to what minimum you need to survive. In other words, if your primary source of income got disrupted, this is what you need when it gets down to the crunch. This is not the goal for your life. This is not an ideal end point. Unless you are sworn to an internal pledge of not enough, this is definitely not where we thrive. The beauty of knowing this number is to see how much you need. Not want. Just need. It's a mental exercise and not to define what your long-term financial goal is.

Enough is that comfortable space where needs are met. Did you know that when given the option of rating our sense of wellness on a scale between 1 and 5, most would choose a 3? We are comfortable with the middle. Wanting more makes us think we are greedy because society has taught us that there is a finite pie. There is scarcity. You don't get to have more than comfortable. What if that's not true? What if settling for just enough is how we get stuck with doing the familiar, the routine, the okay? The key is to define enough for yourself.

It's okay to choose enough and it's also okay to choose beyond enough. When we start to recognize that meeting our needs and wants is already achieved and we can still choose to grow, this happens next. The idea of having money based on our choice for growth and our individual capacity becomes simply exercising our God-given ability to grow into that capacity that already exists for us in our future.

Having more than barely sufficient is a great thing. We need money. Money has an impact. If you have plenty of cash, that will translate into a lot of good in this world. Time is the ultimate goal. Having more money means you get to spend your time how you choose, on your own terms.

LET'S GET STARTED

Kris is a single mom to a beautiful young lady.

As a single mom, taking care of her daughter was a priority to her. Providing a safe environment and spending precious time with her was her priority. She always dreamed of owning a business and wanted more passive income. However, she was the sole source of income. Her fear of losing money and potential change to her sense of security was the reason she maintained the status quo.

Learning to question our own limiting beliefs can be so powerful. Being a single mom and needing a stable source of income was the reason Kris chose not to change. What she came to realize was that being able to create a flexible business and learn how to stop exchanging money for time was of value to her. Being a single mom wasn't why she shouldn't change. Rather, the value of time over money became why she had to.

As a woman physician, there will always be reasons why you think you cannot or should not do what you know you want to do. It may be your relationship status, your past mistakes, the family you were born into, the zip codes you were born into, the color of your skin, your gender, or your country of origin.

Regardless of your reason(s), you can learn how to have money. You are more than capable. I will take it even a step further and say that the reason you may think you are incapable is typically why you really should learn and do what you want to do.

An orange seed will not grow into an apple tree. If you want to grow apples, you plant apple seeds. If you want to grow wealthy, you have to change how you think about money so that you have it, grow it, enjoy it, and use it as the tool it was created to be.

RX SUMMARY

- When talking about money is taboo, we can't effectively advocate for ourselves. Women physicians are consistently paid less than our male counterparts.

- It's expensive to be a doctor. We pay extra for full childcare coverage and have large student loan debts. In addition, our jobs are no longer as secure as they once were, and more and more doctors are suffering from burnout.

- It's okay to want more than enough.

- You are capable of making this change in your life.

CHAPTER 2

Your Personal Money Story

I did not know I wanted to be a gastroenterologist until I was in my third year of medical school. I thought I was going to be a primary care physician or pediatrician.

During my surgery rotation, I found myself spending hours reading about diverticulosis and diverticulitis. Yes, proud nerd here! I didn't even know gastroenterology was a possible field in medicine for me. Most of the physicians I had met who looked like me were mostly in primary care. I wanted to be like them. They were inspirational!

But my love for all things guts and diverticulosis took me down a different path. A path I didn't even know existed.

You are probably thinking, "What the heck? Why is she telling me this story?"

I had never considered gastroenterology before I went to medical school. I was the first physician in my family. My parents were not college educated. My clinical exposure before medical school was limited to primary care settings growing up. I used to contrast this with some of my colleagues who came into medical school knowing exactly what they would be doing, who had grown up with doctors for parents and knew the ins and outs of different kinds of medicine. In a group of almost 150, we all had different experiences growing up.

The same is true for money. Not all hands are created equal.

Our background and upbringing play a significant role in how we view, interpret, and handle money. When thoughts or events happen, we interpret them based on our life's history and we create stories. The mental stories we create build or break our finances.

OUR MONEY STORY

Pauline and Nancy met at a social event organized for new employees at their hospital.

Pauline is an internist. As a young child growing up, she remembers many sleepless nights, worried about whether or not rent was going to be paid. She heard her parents whispering in the one-bedroom apartment they shared as a family of five. She was presumed to be asleep. Her fear was they could end up homeless. They never had conversations about money or investments. She was taught that money was only for adults to discuss. She avoids conversations about money and finds it difficult to ask about what she may not know regarding investments. The stories she tells herself are in the context of her lived experience.

Contrast that with Nancy. She is also an internist. She grew up in a middle-class family. They had generational money that had been passed down from her grandmother. Money was never an issue. They knew they would be fine no matter what. Money and investment conversations were dinnertime discussions. They were easy and normal, and Nancy has no recollection of finance-related strain. As an adult, Nancy feels comfortable having conversations about investment and money. She has renegotiated her income a number of times since starting at their place of work five years ago.

Their varied experience, background, and mindset about money led them through different financial journeys that are currently impacting how they both earn from the same clinical job. Nancy now earned about $50,000 more per year working the same hours.

There seems to be so much stacked against us that unless we are consciously evaluating the impact of the story around our money, we will remain victims of our own circumstances and unhelpful beliefs.

Our money story refers to the mental elaboration of our thoughts and beliefs about money as defined by how we interpret various aspects or events surrounding money and finances. Did you have discussions about money growing up? What was the context of those conversations? The goal of this exercise is not to judge your upbringing but rather understand the effect it plays in how you see money and finances. Did you grow up in a single- or double-earning family? Did you grow up with secure housing or was access to food and shelter limited? Were you taught that money is evil and people with money were perceived as greedy?

Was money a limited commodity? Did your family worry about

money? Was money a constant source of argument in the family or between your parents? Similarly, was there guilt about having money or contempt about not having money?

Some of this is conscious, but most becomes implanted into our own subconscious programming.

Regardless of what that experience was, there are conscious and unconscious lessons that we acquire from our upbringing that impacts our money story as adults. This typically reveals itself in our finances. Just like the quality of a tree is a reflection of the quality of the soil and the fruit.

As women, there are additional factors that affect our money story. The reality is that we live in a postcolonial world where patriarchy and racism affects the opportunities that have been availed to women and minorities. Structural systems in place weren't created with us in mind. Up until the 1970s, women needed their husband's signature to obtain credit cards. In the 1920s, a whole financially thriving African American community in Tulsa was destroyed with white residents given weapons by city officials. Today, Black home owners are at higher risk of having homes underappraised compared to their white counterparts.

Even in medicine, women on average continue to be paid and offered less than their male counterparts. We are less likely to be promoted despite evidence to show that we provide higher quality of care on average.[5]

---

5   Kimber P. Richter et al., "Women Physicians and Promotion in Academic Medicine," *New England Journal of Medicine* 383, no. 22 (2020): 2148–2157, https://doi.org/10.1056/ NEJMsa1916935; Yusuke Tsugawa et al., "Comparison of Hospital Mortality and Readmission Rates for Medicare Patients Treated by Male vs Female Physicians," *JAMA Internal Medicine* 177, no. 2 (2017): 206–213, https://doi.org/10.1001/jamainternmed.2016.7875.

These internal and external forces impact our money story.

Are we then screwed? Are these circumstances irreversible? Do you have your money story until you die, or are you able to let go of the stories that may not work in your favor?

The answer is, of course we can change our money stories. It just takes the hard work of unlearning what we've learned.

CHANGING YOUR MONEY STORY

Kara has been in practice for many years. She runs her own clinical practice and earns what she considers a good income. Despite this, she always worries about money. Her spouse earns a good income as well. This doesn't seem to reassure her enough.

When it comes to spending, she has a fear of running out of money. She feels like she never has enough and constantly worries about running out.

Kara's fears stem from her childhood. She was raised in a two-income family. Her father was very frugal while her mother spent a lot, sometimes at the expense of their core needs. There were years where money was a cause of significant arguments. Eventually, her parents separated.

Unconsciously, she carried along a story of money being the cause of fights. Money causes friction. The less time you spend on money, the lower the chances of fights. Most of these thoughts were not conscious. She also believed spending was bad. Due to her fear of losing money, she found herself hoarding cash because having a large amount of cash made her feel safe. She also didn't invest as much due to her fears. She had to acknowledge the impact of her money story so she could create a different story in line with the life she wanted to create intentionally. She had to learn to replace her old story with a new story and live with that in mind. For instance, "I have to keep my cash so I don't lose money" became "I am losing money by letting it sit in my account without investing."

Your present is the result of your past. Your future becomes the result of beliefs and actions you choose to take today and the imaginative assumptions or conclusions you are making as a result. Your past doesn't get to define your future—unless you let it.

HOW CAN YOU CHANGE YOUR MONEY STORY?

It starts by being aware that your assumptions (especially the imaginative ones) about money may not be the only possible truth about money. Every belief or thought is a sentence in our brain. Our neurons formulated a message. We have an average of 6,000 thoughts per day. We keep some and ditch some. We tend to keep those that feel familiar and safe to us. The thoughts that feel most familiar are those we have been prompted to find familiar based on our history and past.

What if it is possible that we can create a different story—about us, about money, about spending, about wealth?

For instance, you may believe that money is hard. Now, every time you come to a financial crossroad, you subconsciously have this story of how making money is difficult and that is why your net worth is not growing and so forth. The question now becomes, is this story helpful for you today or not?

We cannot change our past about money, but we can start to change how we interpret events. If you missed the deadline to file your taxes, you can start to make that mean you are bad with money. Whereas someone else can interpret it to simply mean they were busy and forgot. One is without judgment. The other is with judgment. Which one is more helpful toward future growth?

We make up stories and choose thoughts that feel familiar. The way to change your money story is by becoming aware of this and choosing thoughts that help you become financially stronger, not weaker.

Here are the steps to changing your money story.

1. Becoming aware.

   Most of us are unaware of the difference between truth and fact compared to a story we are telling ourselves. When we learn to pay more attention to the interpretation we are giving, our sensitivity increases and it becomes easier. A simple question that helps with identification and reframing is this: "Is my assumption true? Is it 100 percent true? Is it always true? Is there any scenario in which this story I am telling myself is not 100 percent the only truth?"

   For instance, as a busy physician mom, I told myself that I was too busy to take care of my finances. That was a story I was telling myself that resulted in me avoiding my finances. But then the reality hit me: every human has twenty-four hours a day, including CEOs of trillion-dollar companies and presidents of countries. The issue must not be that I was too busy. I decided the issue was that I was not creating time.

2. Determine whether your story is helpful.

   Is this story helping you achieve your desired result, or is it keeping you stuck?

   Keeping the time example above, my story about time was keeping me stuck. I had a choice: I could keep it, or I could ditch that story. Why was it important to ditch it? If "I don't have time" was not a thing, meaning if it did not exist, what would I do if I wanted to achieve the outcome of having my finances not look like a hot mess? Here are some of the things I came up with:

   A. Delegate unimportant recurring activities to someone else.

   B. Automate my bills and investments.

   C. Spend one hour less on Netflix per week and instead spend that time doing finance-related activities.

   D. Spend one hour while my kids watch TV on Saturday learning how to invest in real estate.

      The bottom line is that the stories we tell ourselves can become blocks that stop our brains from finding creative ways to get us to our final goals.

3. Find a more helpful story.

   All stories are made up of interpretations of the world as we see it. You can let your own money story limit you, or you can let it liberate you to the next level. The story I chose was that

I had twenty-four hours like everyone else. I am a physician and I can do hard things. I can be brilliant and creative and use time as my ally and not my nemesis.

REST STOP: YOUR MONEY STORY

1. What stories have you been carrying regarding your finances that have been preventing you from achieving the next step in your finances?

2. Do you want to keep them or ditch them?

3. Are you certain?

4. What new stories are you choosing to take along with you to displace the previous unhelpful stories?

To be clear, it can sometimes be difficult to catch your own stories especially if you don't verbalize it. We are too close to our own thoughts that we don't realize they may not be the absolute truth. The more you speak out to yourself or others about your finances, the more opportunities you will have to identify what may be stories (not facts).

YOUR MONEY STORY IS NOT STATIC

As we continue through life, we continue to add on to our story.

Ray was in medical school when her parents lost their home. She had had no official money teaching from them, except if you count the lessons of "what not to do." When she graduated from the fellowship, she knew she had to change how she viewed and managed money, otherwise she would end up in a financial mess.

She already knew that it wasn't all about how much you make but what you do with it that mattered.

For many years, the story she told herself was that money was difficult and money was never going to be enough.

After going through the exercise above, she realized this was a story based on her past. She consciously chose a new story about money. She chose to believe that she was someone who could master money. The fact that her parents didn't have the same belief didn't have to mean the same was true for her.

She was able to remove the mentally locked door that had been limiting her.

She started investing. She diversified her income sources. She went even further by sharing these concepts with her parents. For the first time in her adult life, they became debt-free and now also plan to invest in real estate.

Our money story can change. Our self-empowerment can change our families. It can change family trees.

You may not be able to change the past, but you can change and affect the future.

Who you are today is the result of your journey as you walked and grew through life. Your journey is not good or bad. You may even wish things were different, but fighting with the past doesn't change it. You can choose the habits and beliefs that help you create the result you want, even as an underdog.

You don't have to hate your present in order to choose to grow.

This feels like a new money chapter for women physicians.

Are you ready to dive in and rise?

RX SUMMARY

- We all have our money stories that are the result of our own history and experience through life.

- Identifying and transforming unhelpful stories will help you move toward the financial growth you desire.

CHAPTER 3

Your Relationship
with Money

When I began my journey to financial freedom, my relationship with money was set on ensuring that money wasn't an important factor in determining how I lived my life. The fact that I drew that conclusion should come as no surprise considering how many times we have been taught that money is the root of evil. Subconsciously, I didn't want anything to do with it. I Ignored it or gave it away. Consciously, I wanted to have money, but my subconscious drive was so strong that I didn't even know I was repelling it. The unhealthy part of this was, I was not prepared for any financial emergency. I was not investing or growing my net worth. Heck, I was simply paying the minimum on my student loans.

Money felt uncomfortable.

The good news is that change is completely doable.

We should recognize that our preprogrammed automated patterns are the result of our thoughts about money, which, in turn, become our relationship with it. How we relate with money is very important. Maybe this is the first time you are hearing that there is a relationship between you and your money. It is easy to pretend or attempt to ignore it, but its existence is there regardless.

You might as well become aware so you can optimize money to work for you.

As we have learned in the previous chapter, our money story has a major part to play in our relationship with finances. Our relationship with anything is the set of thoughts that we have about that specific thing. Some of these are conscious and others are subconscious. Part of succeeding and rewriting our money story is bringing the subconscious to the surface so we can become aware of our power to choose and have.

You may think this concept is strange at first glance. What you are actually doing is a better indication of your deep-rooted belief than what you consciously believe.

Sometimes our subconscious beliefs are exactly the opposite of what we want to consciously believe. Unearthing them and realigning them is power.

HEALTHY AND UNHEALTHY RELATIONSHIPS

Imagine the relationship between you and one of your favorite girl-friends. You know each other. You enjoy spending time with each other. After a long week of life, you enjoy talking about how the week went. You listen and share with each other. At the end of your time together, both of you feel nourished and encouraged. Now picture the opposite. Imagine a relationship where whenever you finally have time for a phone call, only one person does all the talking. She doesn't ask how you are doing or how your family is doing. When you don't pick up a call or text back immediately, she feels uncertain about if you are still friends. She doesn't ever seem to come with good news. It's always about her and how you can be of service to her. Her needs only.

If you replace favorite girlfriends with a significant other, the same point carries over.

Take a moment and imagine an ideal relationship with a significant other. What does an ideal relationship look like?

Are you hoarding each other? Are you giving each other room to breathe? Do you understand the power each person has? Are you letting those around you experience the goodness that exists in your partner? Are you relying on them to define you, elevate you, make you feel worthy? The same questions apply to money. It was never meant to define you, elevate you, or make you feel worthy.

Similarly, you and money thrive better together when you have a healthy space between you. Financial growth isn't what you center your life on, and your personal growth isn't defined by what is happening in your bank or investment accounts only.

One of my favorite passages in the Bible states, "Love is patient. Love is kind." I also like to add that love is breathable. Your money grows better when you let it grow. It's hard for money to grow when you are holding on to it with a chokehold.

A negative relationship with money can take many forms. Here are a few of the most common.

HOLDING ON

Watching it closely in our savings account because we don't want to lose it is the simplest, most common way we slowly let money slip away because of the power of inflation. We feel safer having the money in a savings account. Some of our foremothers used to put money in bras and under pillows. It won't grow. In fact, the inflation rate averages between 2 percent and 9 percent. As I write this book during the pandemic, it's around 9 percent. If your money is making less than that, you are losing money. Money that's not been used or stamped for an acute or subacute use should be out on the streets working for you, not being held tight in your hand.

But what if you lose some money? Will your life be practically over? Are you completely indifferent? Are you extremely scared about that possibility? Do you think it is not ideal, but you know you will be okay regardless? Many of us are afraid to lose money because of the feared loss of security. This fear may be more pronounced if you grew up with a sense of lack. It may be that money and what you are able to get with it has become part of your self-identity. In that case, losing it may feel like losing a limb or self.

MONEY AS A SOURCE OF VALUE

Another way we misalign our relationship with money is in how we use it. Many of us use it as a way to prove our qualifications or acceptance. We think the presence or absence of money is an indication of one's worth or value. Your value is innate. It has nothing to do with what you own, earn, or have. When we realize that our value or worth is not something that diminishes, we start to see money simply as a feature that augments.

You have incredible value that has nothing to do with what you do because your dollar amount (whether high or low) isn't a measure of your value as a human. Your value was maximized the moment you were born. All babies do is pee, poop, cry, play, feed, and keep us up at night. Yet, their value isn't any less. Unfortunately in this patriarchal world where women and minorities can be seen as less than, it is not surprising that we have internalized some of this as well. The world says when you have money, you have value. When you don't, you are less. This is a lie that is all around. We have to see the lie, recognize it, and be willing to stand against this grain so we can do differently and create a world for future generations where the structures of colonialism aren't defining our world.

We already see how it plays out. Let's try a different experiment.

WEALTH IS IMMORAL

Grace grew up on a reservation. Her family was considered middle class. They always had enough to eat, some extras, and were comfortable. She contrasted this with some of her friends on the reservation with more limited funds. Growing up, she and her friends had heard stories of the wealthy taking from them. Land was taken from her ancestors. These stories stayed with her. Now, as a practicing physician, the idea of having money felt like a scratch against the blackboard. She was subconsciously averse. Because to her, wealth is immoral and taken from a group or person with less.

This is not a rare experience. Many of us have images of some bigger, aggressive person or group taking from someone less, sometimes by force.

How can we change the narrative if you stay out of the game? How do we change the future for our kids if we continue to teach consciously and subconsciously that having money is bad? For instance, conveying the message that "you don't want to have too much."

What we need is more money in the hands of those who intend to use money as a tool to augment and create good in the world. That way, we can unleash it into the spaces in need of change. As an example, a knife can be used to make delicious meals or can be used to wage a fight. It's the hand that holds it that directs the power.

I believe money is a tool for good. Just like water, it takes the shape of its container.

Money doesn't change you; it reveals you. Humans change, period. With or without money. This is why in order to become the kind of wealthy-minded physician who will change the future of medicine, you have to commit to knowing who you are from the inside. Wealth is built first from the inside and then from outside.

SHAME AND GUILT

Shame is one of the least helpful emotions when it comes to money. It prevents us from moving past what we may have perceived as errors or mistakes. It is usually based on a thought that you should know better or should have done differently when, in fact, our mistakes are the cost of our lesson. Mistakes are life's tuition. When we start to understand that we shouldn't aim to avoid mistakes completely but rather be willing to learn and pivot, we can release the shame. What if your experience was exactly what should have happened? You can't change the past. You can't go through life constantly "should-ing."

Angela lost money in an investment years ago. Since then, she has become very cautious. She has her money sitting in a savings account and she's afraid of making financial mistakes again. She carries a lot of shame and guilt about her previous experience. Letting financial mistakes cause us to throw in the towel is like a physician quitting medicine at the first error. An "attendier" attending is one who has made mistakes and chosen to learn and pivot. It's how their game got so strong.

Which one would you rather be: an attendier attending or a new attending who has never made any mistakes? Every financially successful human has lost money at some point. Yes, that's not the goal. But the more you learn that it's part of the process, the more liberated you will be.

A HEALTHY RELATIONSHIP

An ideal, healthy relationship between you and your money can exist. It is freeing. Imagine letting your money breathe, letting it go to places far from you. When you invest it, you let it out of your grasp. As I like to say, money likes company. When you let it go away through investing and giving wisely, it comes back to you. The amazing thing is that it comes back with its cousins, siblings, and friends.

Money augments, not defines. It accentuates; it does not create. This is very important to understand. When you are running parallel with your money and detaching your value from your net worth, you will manage your finances in a way that is liberating.

You will handle it with freedom in a way that lets it grow without the attachment to your worth.

You are also less likely to overspend, less likely to feel shame about your decisions, and also more likely to invest freely and more aggressively. Whether you lose or win, you already won. Done!

When you have a healthy, kind, freeing relationship with money, you get to create the financial life of your dreams. You deserve it, but it starts from the inside out.

REST STOP: WHAT IS YOUR RELATIONSHIP WITH MONEY?

1. What kind of relationship do you currently have with money? What kind of relationship do you desire? Many of us never decide this intentionally.

2. Take a few minutes to write this down.

YOUR RELATIONSHIP WITH YOURSELF: IT ALWAYS STARTS WITH YOU

Katherine and I had been working together on her money and relationship. At the end of one of our sessions, I asked what her thoughts were about herself. She gave a long list of what she liked, but one thing stood out: most of her list was based on what she had done. The doing, not the being. When we love our state of being not due to what we have accomplished but just based on who we are, true magic starts to happen.

Have you ever tried to strike up a conversation with someone you just met? The first thing we tend to ask is, "What do you do?"

It's no wonder we define ourselves by what we do. A different approach is asking a simple open-ended question such as "What do you like to do? Tell me about yourself."

I assigned Katherine to write a letter to herself. In the letter, she was to write down everything she liked and loved about herself. She described it as one of the most powerful things she had done.

REST STOP: A LETTER TO YOU

1. Take a piece of paper/writing material.

2. Write a letter to the present you but coming from your eighty-year-old self. What would you tell yourself she loved about you today? In what ways is she proud of you right now?

3. Write a letter to your current self from your fourteen-year-old self. Let her tell you what she loves about you and what in what specific ways she is proud of you today. Remember to write not just what you have done but who you are.

Just as you have a relationship with money, we all have relationships with ourselves. When it comes to money, we are the CEOs of our financial lives. The CEO can make or break a company. If a CEO doesn't see their own power or they lack the core qualities of a leader, you can imagine the implications.

A leader doesn't have to be the most knowledgeable part of the team in every aspect. But they do have to be confident enough, humble enough, and have the foundations needed to recognize and retain talent. You can't see or know talent unless you have your own foundational piece on point.

How you see yourself is the root of your success. Regardless of your past or what your brain is telling you, you can learn to become more aware and change the status quo relationship with yourself if the current one isn't creating the result you want.

Someone once asked me what my favorite book was. I referred back to a children's book titled, *I Like Myself.* Listen, I don't care how old you are. If you don't at least like yourself, it's hard to have the financial life of your dreams. You will always spend, save, and even invest from a place of deficit. You will be trying to work from an empty cup. It just ain't gonna work. It may work for a season, but if you are reading this book, it means you want to create a bigger impact in a way that is healthy and breathable. You are a part of that equation. The goal is to love yourself. Not just what you do or what you create but simply who you are. Money becomes easy, fun, and less stressful.

You cannot build the kind of wealth you want without transforming your relationship with yourself. You cannot transform your relationship with yourself without first knowing yourself. You need to develop self-like, self-love, self-compassion, and the ability to have your own back no matter what.

You have to embrace the abundance of love, trust, money, and opportunities. You have to trust and see your ability to be resourceful. You don't have "just one shot"!

Before she wrote the letter to herself, Katherine didn't feel good about the money stuff. She had the cash but had the money worries still. How you think about money is just a reflection of how you think about other things. If you worry about money, you are likely worried about other things. If you don't trust yourself when it comes to money, it is possible that you don't trust yourself about other things as well. Doing this exercise has increased her trust in herself and ability to take financial actions, including finally starting the investments she has been postponing for years.

In our money coaching community, we start with our relationships with ourselves. Because money and struggles with money are rarely ever about money itself. Having money will help you buy things and get things, but money itself won't change you. If you are unhappy without it, you will not be happy with it. If you are uncertain without money, you will be uncertain with money. The key is to grow yourself in this journey. Love yourself at least most of the time, and see that you are already enough. Remember that you are already a badass. It's your baseline.

REMEMBER, YOU'RE A BADASS

Jane is a married physician. For many years, she had avoided looking at her finances. By the time we met, she was ready to empower herself and change how she felt about her finances. As part of her knowing the details of her finances, she and her husband decided to meet up with a potential financial advisor for a one-time consultation to get an overview of their investment plans. The advisor kept on addressing her husband. He avoided speaking to her directly and instead focused only on her husband. Halfway through their consultation, he found out she was a physician. He exclaimed to her, "You know physicians are bad with money." She admitted that her previous self would have embarrassingly agreed with him. Not anymore. She spoke up and made the decision to not hire him as part of her financial team.

Luckily, Jane had been working on her relationship with herself and with money, so she didn't let herself get emotional about the way that financial advisor had treated her. Regardless of your history, it is important to know that you can develop and create new, different, and more optimal relationships that are based on what you want to create in the future and not based on past wounds.

And Jane's first step? She knew her own badassery. If nothing else, remember this:

As women physicians, we are badass at what we do every day. We see patients and come up with a crazy differential diagnosis in the middle of unethically short clinical visits. We go through crazy long medical training. We perform surgery and procedures, we put needles in holes that are crazy. Yet, when it comes to money, we choose to believe things like "Money is hard."

The only reason money will seem hard is that we simply have forgotten who we are.

We are badasses. We can do anything we set our minds to. We know how to do the near impossible. We set out to be physicians in a process that takes at least seven years. We know how to harness the power of delayed gratification. Yes, we are badasses.

Start to see yourself as someone who has the capacity to do wonderful things with money. You are a great steward of it.

When we realize that liking ourselves is not negotiable, we stop asking ourselves if (or how much) money can bring happiness. One has nothing to do with the other. Yes, this may unearth some unaddressed trauma, but honestly, not addressing those is already affecting your life's experience and wealth. The most productive thing to do may be to start now.

FIND YOUR MONEY MANTRA

My thought about money is this: "I am resourceful. I can always build again. Money doesn't define me. I am not more amazing with or without. I choose to have and use it for so many amazing things and impact. If I lose it, I will build it again."

We can call this my money mantra. What do you want yours to be? Write it out. Read it every day. Think about it. Let it marinate into your bones so you can feel it. The more you feel it, the more you believe it. The deeper it sinks.

These thoughts are a result of my relationship with money and myself. It wasn't always that way.

REST STOP: MONEY MANTRA

1. What do you want to believe about yourself and money? This is your money mantra.

2. What is your money mantra?

Write it out.

Feel it.

Practice it until it becomes second nature to you.

Visit www.moneyfitmd.com/worksheet for sample mantras you can use as inspiration as you create your own.

When I started my money journey, money felt like hot potatoes to me. "Don't touch it. Stay away from it. Avoid it." It took intentionality work (as detailed here) to create a healthier relationship. When you see the downstream effect on how you show up, how you live your life, and how you practice medicine, you will see that failing to take the time to intentionally create a healthier relationship is the ultimate waste of the precious life we have.

RX SUMMARY

1. A knife can be used to make delicious meals or can be used to wage a fight. It's the hand that holds it that directs the power. Just like the knife, money can be a tool for good. It takes directions from the holder.

2. Money augments; it doesn't define.

3. Remember that you're already a badass! Now let's unleash that badass energy on your money.

CHAPTER 4

Spending Myth

In the last months of fellowship, two of the most common questions I was asked were "What house are you buying?" and "What purse are you buying?" All of the soon-to-be doctors, including me, were excited about the prospect of an increased paycheck and all the things we'd soon be able to buy for ourselves.

In contrast, when I began my journey to figuring out my money life, the first thing I was told to do was stop spending. The advice I kept hearing was, "Start 'no spend' months."

"Spending is bad for your net worth." "The more you spend the less you have."

I dialed in on that. I kept the receipts on everything. Anytime I spent, it felt like I was failing at something. I even considered using an envelope method of monitoring my spending.

I figured, the less you spend, the more you have, correct? Wrong! Thank God I realized very quickly that there were other ways of managing money. I spend more now than ever before and my net worth keeps growing.

Everyone spends. Spending by itself is not good or bad. What you spend on is the key thing. I'm not talking about the "coffee will make you broke" gospel either.

First things first. How come no one talks to us about spending in a wealthy way? Spending is something we all do. Yet, when we get financial advice, it usually only goes as far as "Stop overspending. Get a budget."

Seriously, that is the biggest disservice ever.

To be clear, there is nothing fundamentally wrong with spending versus not spending. However, what I discovered was that you can only cut your spending so much. As I learned more about money and explored circles where money was discussed in intimate settings, here is what I discovered: These people were not spending less, yet their net worth grew exponentially. This knowledge has led me to the conclusion that spending less is not the solution.

What you spend on is what matters.

Let's dig in a little more.

Consider the case of two physicians. They both have the same amount of take-home pay.

Doctor A spends about 80 percent of her take-home pay. She was raised by a single mom who understood the importance of spending well. With every paycheck, she automated her investments.

Doctor B spends 60 percent of her take-home pay. She was taught that money is very important. So important, in fact, that you don't want to lose it. She prefers to hold her post-expenses money in her savings account.

Which one of these fictional doctors would you rather be?

Yes, this is a simplified and hypothetical scenario.

Doctor A may have less cash left, but most of her spending is in investments. This is well defined by *Rich Dad, Poor Dad*. Assets put money in your pocket or grow your net worth while liabilities dip your net worth. Examples of assets include cash-flowing rental investments, income-generating stock investments, bonds, Treasury bills, co-ownership or partnership in income-generation businesses, and patents. The key to spending well is to spend more on assets before liabilities. Alternatively, buy assets, get your cash flow from it, and then pay for liabilities with that.

Simply put, net worth is your assets minus your liability. Therefore, if you are spending mostly on liabilities, you will tend toward a lower positive (or even negative) net worth relative to where you would be, based on your income source. If your income is going primarily toward buying assets, then your net worth will tend more toward a higher positive.

Screening through the high-quality versus low-quality wealth items lens can also help differentiate whether you're spending with a wealth mindset or a poverty mindset. Low-quality wealth items don't build your net worth or sense of wealth. Examples of high-quality wealth items include investing in coaching, buying assets, giving, and improving your net worth over the long haul.

Examples of low-quality wealth items include low-quality clothing or personal accessories that require frequent replacement and long-term higher overall cost. Even big-ticket items such as cars or your primary home can be low-quality wealth items if the required payments are more expensive than you can easily afford without derailing your long-term plans.

YOU CAN'T BUDGET YOUR WAY TO WEALTH

Mary is a board-certified dermatologist. I met her during a guest coaching visit I did in a program. She had been trying to get her financial house in order. In fact, she has purchased a popular budgeting system called YNAB (You Need a Budget). It is arguably one of the most sophisticated platforms, but she had been struggling with using YNAB due to the steep learning curve required. It can take a few months to get completely accustomed to the system. She was so focused on this step that everything else was at a standstill. She was not diversifying her income, and she was not investing. It almost seemed like she assumed "once I get this off the ground, then I can have money."

After our session together, she saw how this was a limiting block and was delaying the more important work. The next day, she ditched YNAB and started using Mint. Once she released the roadblock of the perfect budgeting system, she started taking action beyond budgeting.

If I had a penny for how many times I hear women looking for the best way to budget, I would be way past millionaire status. It's almost as if we think that the perfect budgeting system will create wealth. I have news for you. I hope it's good news. Budgeting apps and budgeting systems by themselves do not create wealth.

Amateurs think the tool is the most essential. Professionals know the tool is just a tool. How you use it is the most critical. A budgeting system is a spending plan that should tell you where your money is going. It's like creating an army of minions that you are directing based on your values.

You see, many of us treat "budgeting" like a very complex calculus when it's simply a plan or recipe to ensure we are spending in a way that lights us up. Regardless of where you are, spending well is the goal. You may start in a place of hating how you spend. You may have shame or guilt about it. Simply know that your current spending is the result of decisions made in the past. But you get to choose how you want to feel when you see your statement next month.

Decide. Fix it or ditch it.

SPEND ON ASSETS, NOT LIABILITIES

Marg is a physician. She makes a good income as a psychiatrist. However, she feels like she never has anything left at the end of the month. Most of her expenses feel important to her and she never felt like she was splurging in any way. After reviewing her expenses, she reported that she liked how she was spending and didn't have any negative emotions about what she was spending on.

For many physicians, we tend to experience lifestyle creep. Meaning that as we earn more, we tend to spend more. Without intentionality, this may end up being low-quality wealth items or liabilities. Spending in itself isn't bad or good. In fact, the less judgmental we are about money, the better. The question is, are you getting the result you want or not?

For Marg, since she likes where her money was going on a superficial level, the next question was if she was spending more on assets or on liabilities. The key isn't to judge where one is. The key is to ask if the result is what we want it to be. Is she getting the financial outcome she desired? For her, the answer was no. This encouraged her to redirect the flow of her money. She still spends on liabilities but spends more on assets. Her net worth is growing. She really, really loves her spending now because she knows that it's exactly what her version of a badass spends like.

REST STOP: ASSETS VERSUS LIABILITIES

1. Are you spending more on liabilities or are you spending more on assets?

2. What percentage of your spending is on high-quality wealth items versus low quality?

3. What do your spending habits tell about your story and what you value?

As women physicians, we are mostly taught that spending is bad. Many of us have taken this so closely to heart that it has become ingrained in us. Spend less, have more. It's no wonder we struggle and miss out on investment opportunities because we feel uncomfortable spending.

The whole idea of spending less is based on the patriarchal assumption that women are more likely to spend on liabilities while men spend on assets. Financial education content geared toward women talks about spending and budgeting while male-focused content talks more about investment.[6] You reading this means we are changing the narrative.

The first step is always awareness. Now you are aware.

When it comes to money, many of us are quick to brag about how little we spend. We have been conditioned to feel shame about spending. The larger, the more shame. "Brag about how little you are spending. Brag about how much you are saving." This is not what men are taught. They brag about how much they spend and what they invest in and rarely talk about how much they save. Yes, this is generalizing, but the pattern is true. It's no wonder they tend to have a higher net worth.

If we can spend more on assets and less on liability, our net worth will grow. In essence, spend more, have more. But the key is what you spend on.

WHY DO WE SPEND WHAT WE SPEND?

Joan is a married physician. She had been married for ten years. Overall, she felt like her relationship was mostly a happy one, but she wondered why it seemed like she was living paycheck to paycheck. She decided to investigate by looking at her spending. She noticed a spike in her spending whenever there was an argument with her spouse. It wasn't something she was doing consciously. However, whenever she felt sad, shopping made her feel better. By itself, this wasn't dangerous as an isolated event. However, if done repeatedly, this spending pattern could impact her finances. Part

6   Russia Trust Fund for Financial Literacy and Education, *Women and Financial Literacy: OECD/INFE Evidence, Survey and Policy Responses* (June 2013), https://www.oecd.org/daf/fin/financial-education/TrustFund2013_OECD_INFE_Women_and_Fin_Lit.pdf.

of our strategy together was learning to decrease spending during seasons that she might be feeling emotional. This is referred to as emotional spending.

When it comes to spending or purchasing, there is a reason we spend the way we do.

Are you spending to distract from an emotion you are avoiding? This is called buffering. Buffering refers to the act of spending, buying, or doing something to distract or decrease the intensity of an emotion.

Many of our actions or inactions are fueled by our feelings. We do certain things when we are happy and others when we are not. We do certain things when we feel shame and avoid others. I find one of the most common reasons that we ignore or avoid our finances as physicians is related to emotions such as shame and discomfort. Not all these emotions are negative. Some are positive but may still lead to unwanted results. For instance, why does celebrating have to lead to overspending? How about celebrating fully and letting ourselves feel the completeness of that emotion?

As humans, we have been taught that emotions can be danger-ous. If it does not feel good, avoid it. This avoidance can have a significant impact on our spending and investment and is one of the reasons why I am a huge fan of automating the recurrent actions you intend to take. Our feelings can lead to inactions and actions that can negatively impact our finances.

Getting comfortable with feeling our emotions is critical to grow-ing wealth, taking calculated risks, and avoiding overspending. When working with clients, I remind them that feelings are the vibration of nerves in our body. Never in the history of humanity have emotions killed by themselves. Nonetheless, we resist emotion and try to avoid it, and that is the real cause of the negative or unwanted effects.

When we embrace the nonlethality of our emotions, we will be able to embrace the full experience of life. Pro tip: The more I mastered the art of accepting chance I may feel crappy 50 percent of the time, the more my net worth grew, the more my business grew, and the more comfortable I was asking for things I wanted because the worst I could get was a no and the worst that could happen was simply a nerve vibration in my body.

SPEND LIKE A WEALTHY PERSON

Mira is a physician. As the first in her family to become a physician, there were a lot of expectations from her family on what a physician was going to live like, such as fancy houses, cars, extravagant vacations. These expectations had been ingrained in her for so long that by the time she was done with training, her goal was to get a big house. Her three children needed space to be comfortable, or at least that's what she had learned.

Unfortunately, due to her student loan burden, she knew something had to give. Mira had to learn how to spend differently in order for her finances to change. In order to grow her money and net worth, she had to learn to spend wealthily. This meant spending on buying assets that put money into her pocket and increased her net worth. Simultaneously, she decreased spending on things that decreased her net worth.

She had thought all spending was created equal. Her focus now is spending more on assets than liabilities. Anytime she finds her spending creeping more toward liabilities, she can course correct.

When we spend, what we pay is the cost. What we get is the value. The value is what you perceive as the benefit you are getting in exchange for the cash spent. Depending on how you were raised and the experiences you have picked up over the course of your life's journey, you may have been taught to see value in things that may not grow in value. When I was a little girl, I remember my younger sister crying once because she wanted money. She insisted on getting the equivalent of a dollar. My dad had only five dollars with him. She didn't want the $5 bill because she perceived the $1 bill to be of value. My parents eventually found her a dollar. She's now a grown woman and still denies she ever refused a higher dollar amount.

How we are raised affects how we perceive value. Regardless of the past, you can choose to retrain your eyes and your brain. You can choose to see value in assets. You can choose to appreciate delayed gratification on your wealth journey. Instant gratification may be the result of the little burst of dopamine we get as a result of that stimulus. It's akin to the glucose spike with a high-glycemic-content food or snack. It may feel good in the short term, but you know you will pay for it later.

If you have ever suffered from lack, you may be used to spending the least amount possible on things. A low-quality jacket may function for a season. A higher-quality jacket may function for many seasons. That quality difference can come with a price tag. It is best to view cumulative value over the course of the lifetime of the product or service.

Depending on how accustomed you are to prioritizing liabilities, you may need a transitional period to unlearn what you have been taught. That way, you spend and your net worth grows.

How can you know how to spend? Spend based on your values.

REST STOP: THE SPENDING MIRROR

1. If all I had to tell me about you was your account, what would it tell me about you?

   Will it represent the things you say you find valuable?

2. Everything in your account spent is the result of perceived value in the past or unconscious spending. Looking at your spending, would you make those same decisions again? Yea or nay? If not, what will you change?

3. If you find yourself feeling okay with everything on there, go deeper.

4. Are you spending mostly on assets and high-quality wealth items or liabilities and low-quality wealth items? Is that congruent with your goals in this season?

5. If yes, hallelujah!

6. If not, what can you change?

7. Six months from now, will you be glad you spent in this way or will you wish you had the money back?

Spending is a necessary part of our life. As women, it is important that we not globally avoid spending but instead we direct our focus toward spending in a way that builds wealth.

RX SUMMARY

1. Love your spending; decrease emotional variance or reward associated with spending.

2. You can't budget your way to wealth. Don't stop spending. Make your spending work for you!

3. Assets grow your net worth. Increase your spending on assets and decrease your spending on liabilities.

4. When spending on liabilities, think about the value over the lifetime of the product. Spend with a wealth mindset and pay more up front to pay less later.

CHAPTER 5

Debt: From Burden to Leveraged

Growing up in Nigeria, I was told debt was bad. There were no credit cards back then. You could take loans from large banks but typically only if backed by collateral. If you wanted to borrow from a bank, you would need physical collateral such as parcels of land. If you broke the conditions of the contract signed, the bank could legally keep the collateral. However, the world is definitely more evolved now. At age eighteen, I got introduced to credit cards. I was told it's this amazing thing you can use to buy things and simply pay the minimum monthly payment. Although I still maintained a level of discipline, I had no problem using my credit card. I didn't quite understand the compounding nature of the interest I was paying. I also missed the fact that most minimum monthly payments didn't do much to decrease the principal. I could buy anything I wanted, even if I couldn't afford it right away.

This experience is similar to the lessons many people got around debt. Unfortunately, many individuals are taught to use debt to buy liabilities which negatively impacts their finances. However, the wealth-minded think about debt and how to use it differently.

Debt is a tool that can be wagered for "good" or for "bad," just like anything else.

How can you utilize it well and effectively?

First, let's define debt: it is money you borrow because you either don't have the money or you are choosing to not use your money. Typically, it comes with interest. Interest is the cost you pay to have that thing. We typically interpret debt differently depending on how we were raised since surroundings mold our interpretation.

For instance, debt was used by the wealthy to build wealth. However, many lower income families used debt for essentials, for liabilities that didn't compound positively. Debt was offered in the form of payday loans to provide ways for the poor to buy more liabilities. Liabilities are typically made by the wealthy subclass, meaning these liabilities are assets to the companies creating or selling them.

Then came the likes of Dave Ramsey, a well-known financial educator. He set out to teach middle America that debt was bad. Avoid credit cards. Pay cash. Use envelopes. Ramsey's system may work for many people, but as women physicians, it can be limiting and restrictive.

When I began my money journey, I thought that debt was bad, reasoning, "You better pay it off stat so you can finally have peace of mind." Thinking debt is bad has left many women physicians focusing only on debt payoff and not on how to build wealth.

RETHINK YOUR DEBT MINDSET

I met Margaret during a guest coaching appearance. She was exhausted from working extra shifts. She really wished she could spend more time with her children. Her primary thought was that she would work very hard for a few years, pay off her debt, and cut back. She was tired! She was not seeing much of her six-year-old sons. She hoped it would all be worth it when she was done paying off debt. She hoped when she had no more debt, she could work less. Her eyes were focused on only one goal for now. She picked up extra shifts and worked long shifts with the goal of being blissfully happy after paying her debt off. In her words, "It was like a heavy load preventing [her] from enjoying [her] family life." She was tired, burned out, and depressed. She wished things could be different. She wished she didn't carry such a burden and often felt guilty about picking up extra shifts.

To be clear, it was not the debt that was preventing her from spending time with her family. It was her fear and thoughts about the debt itself. If she wasn't carrying such a burden as a result of her fear, she would pace herself better. Without the fear, Margaret could take fewer extra shifts and have more joy in the moment and ultimately less burnout. She would be giving herself the gift of practicing medicine for longer.

I don't recommend keeping your debt forever like it's the family's favorite pet. However, running a marathon at full steam will only cause us to break down.

We have been groomed to despise debt so much. I hear phrases like "It's suffocating." We have to be aware that thoughts such as this can contribute to burnout and unwellness. When you think your debt is suffocating, you are more likely to run toward any perceived lesser threat such as an abusive work environment, unhealthy work hours, or failing to start that business. All because of a thought: my debt is suffocating.

Debt by itself is a neutral circumstance. You get to choose your thoughts about it. Learning to not despise your debt may in fact help you pay it off faster and help you be healthier. That was the case with me. Decreasing my fury against debt meant working breathable hours, sleeping well, and overall less fatigue. I had time to recover between clinical shifts and spend time with my family. This meant less burnout, which can increase longevity in medicine. We also know stress, insomnia, relationship stress, and guilt from overworking can all be associated with overspending. For me, this meant working toward less emotional or stress-induced overspending, which, in turn, gave me more cash to pay off my debt without working extra shifts or weekends that I didn't want to work.

PRODUCTIVE DEBT

Sal was up for partnership in her practice. She knew this day was coming and had saved about $150,000. When the time came, she found out she could get a loan with a low interest rate of about 2 percent. She knew she could get more value from her money than the cost of the interest on the debt.

She chose to take the loan and set up an automatic bimonthly payment from her paycheck. She used her saved-up cash as down payment for an investment property that was cash flowing. The equity is growing. The home is being paid down using money paid by her tenants. This is the power of leverage. She maintained a six-month emergency fund that she could access if needed.

Sal's net worth has grown significantly due to her calculated strategy.

All debts are not created equal.

You cannot keep being afraid of debt.

You have to master it, leverage it, and use it to build your net worth.

This does not mean you keep the debt forever. It means you take a healthier approach. Like some of my clients, you may end up paying it off sooner.

By now, you know an asset puts money in your pocket while liabilities take money out of your pocket. Understanding that debt can be used to leverage wealth building is key. Some call it good debt versus bad debt. Personally, I believe in removing judgment from money. A more preferable term is "productive" versus "nonproductive" debt. Productive debt increases your net worth and moves you toward your goal while nonproductive debt decreases your net worth or takes you away from your goal.

If I purchase a primary home with a down payment versus buying a cash-flowing investment property for the same amount, which one is ideal? It depends on your goals. However, if the goal is wealth building, leveraging debt to buy assets is ideal. A primary home doesn't put money into my pocket in the short term; therefore, it is a liability in the short term. However, if the value increases over time, it can increase my net worth. The caution with this is assuming that the value of the primary home will increase over time. As we know, that is not a linear process. External economic forces affect the value of properties. An investment property that doesn't cover its own monthly expense can also be a liability. An investment property where the rent collected covers the expenses and leaves extra money monthly can be an asset. Same down payment, same amount of debt, different quality of outcomes and effect on net worth.

The question then becomes, how do you feel okay with debt? Or how do you learn to feel less negative so you can leverage it to build wealth?

We can build wealth by using debt to buy assets. This is the beauty of leveraging. Leveraging is when you use borrowed capital to buy an investment with the expectation that the return on investment or profit will be higher than the cost of acquiring the loan or debt. Sal applied the power of leverage when she used a loan to buy an income-producing property. Overleveraging occurs when you stretch the risk-reward to the point of having a very thin margin. It can also be used to describe situations when your borrowing is so high that you are unable to make the payment in the case of an emergency situation, which can be dangerous. Therefore, be sure to have a cushion or emergency funds that can cover your expenses if needed.

Debt is not bad. Using debt to primarily buy liabilities is the caution. Overleveraging debt is the caution. Debt builds wealth. Debt can be a source of freedom and future growth.

Let's change the narrative so we can close some of the wealth gap that exists.

PRACTICE DEBT GRATITUDE

Bryn is a practicing nephrologist. She has been in practice for ten years. Her first employee position was in a toxic environment. She was bullied by the practice administrators. The stress began to affect her health. She dreaded going to work every day. It began to affect her relationship at home. She found herself becoming more short with her children. The limited time she spent with them became filled with annoyance, followed by guilt.

She began overspending and avoiding her finances. About three years into this job, she had an opportunity to buy a practice. To do so, she needed a business loan. Within a year, her practice began making money. This is an example of how debt can help with freedom.

Yet, she hated the debt. Like many, she believed debt was bad. After coaching, she replaced her feeling of hatred with gratitude. That seemed more fitting.

Bryn says, "My debt helped provide me with freedom." Her sigh of relief was palpable. With the relief and clarity of mind, she has been able to create a payment plan that will eliminate the debt sooner than planned and without the additional stress, shame, and guilt. She is doing it like a boss! Calculated. She chose to see she had other choices, including staying in a toxic job. In a world where burnout and physician suicide is at a high, I applaud her resourcefulness in using a business loan.

As physicians, many of us have student debt. Without it, many of us wouldn't be physicians today. I'm grateful for it. It served me well. When I decided it was no longer serving me, I came up with a payoff plan. Hating your loans is optional.

You get to choose how you use debt. You get to choose how you think about it. However, women and people of color are more likely to be taught that debt is bad and should be avoided at all cost. The wealthy are taught that debt creates wealth and is a tool for leveraging.

You choose.

RX SUMMARY

1. Feeling neutral or less negative about your debt doesn't make you keep it. Learning to process debt from a place of gratitude may be the seed that prevents overwhelm and overwork and creates choices.

2. Borrowing to buy assets, aka leveraging, can help build wealth at a faster rate than paying debt off alone or slowly saving the cash to be able to buy 100 percent of the asset from the start. However, being cautious to avoid overleveraging is wise.

3. Stop being afraid of debt. Instead, remember you can be someone who can master it and use it well. When you choose to be free of the baggage of preconceived generational fear of debt, you can make choices from a place of power.

CHAPTER 6

From Saving to Investing

When I was growing up, my family would visit our grandparents in rural southern Nigeria, specifically Ijebu Omu. When bargaining at the markets, women would be seen bringing money they had hidden in their bras. The traditional attires back then didn't have pockets. It was also not rare to hear stories of people keeping money under pillows or in boxes in the ground. That may sound crazy compared to what you are used to. But how does it differ from putting it in a checking account with 1 percent interest?

No real monetary growth happens in bras, pillows, or piggy bank alternatives, and no real growth happens in checking accounts.

I have met many women physicians. Many of them know that having money is important. To some, saving comes easy. However, the fear of investing and fear of making mistakes has limited so much financial growth capacity.

When I met Riley, she was too embarrassed to tell me how much cash she had sitting in her bank account. She works hard. Her mother taught her that saving money was important. But that was where things stopped. Her financial education was incomplete and she lacked the confidence and knowledge to decide what to do next.

She knew she was losing money by letting it all sit in her bank account, not working for her.

Many of us fear investing and losing money in investments. I don't want to lose money either. However, we have to understand that losing money is a possible risk every astute investor has to accept. This shouldn't stop us from investing. In general, there is an inverse relation between risk and return. The more risky (typically), the higher the chances of return. The less risky, the lower the chance of higher growth.

Disparities in wealth exist for many reasons, including our fear of investing. When we don't invest, when we don't think outside of the "savings and pay-off-your-debt box" that women have been placed in, we become part of maintaining the status quo that hasn't served women and people of color especially.

Saving is noble. Investing that saving is wise.

WHEN TO SAVE

Kaima is the head of her household. Her long-term partner was a stay-home parent who was in charge of running the household and homeschooling their four children. After twelve years of being in the same clinical practice, she was now partner and knew that her source of income was relatively secure.

She and her partner had bought their home ten years earlier. At any time, the roof could be in need of a replacement. She also knew that as primary breadwinner, it was important to ensure that there were funds for other emergencies that may occur. She had saved six months of their living expenses in a low-interest-generating savings account at her local credit union. Knowing that money was there if needed gave her a sense of calm and preparedness.

Her next financial plan was to partner with a colleague in buying a franchise of a popular favorite local bakery. She was saving up her cash to have down payment needed for that endeavor.

Kaima is a great example of saving for specific reasons. This doesn't mean she can anticipate everything that can happen. However, it's never a matter of if—there will be an emergency. It is a matter of when and how much. She focused on saving an appropriate amount based on anticipated future needs, while at the same time maintaining a healthy emergency fund for unanticipated emergencies.

Many of us feel good seeing money in the bank account. Maybe it provides a level of security mentally. There is nothing wrong with having a stash of funds, but if you have a large stash sitting in your bank account, you'd better have a larger money army already working for you.

Many times, this sense of security comes from how we were raised. We discussed this earlier. The power of our upbringing affects our sense of security or lack thereof. You may have been taught that dollars provide security. That may be partially true. However, what if it's possible for your sense of security to not be attached to a number but based on your trust in your resourcefulness and ability to create if needed. That way, regardless of that number, you are free to unleash and release your money into the works so it can create more money. Money likes company. It goes where you send it and brings its relatives and friends back to you. Money sitting in a savings account does not do that.

Your money represents little armies. Imagine having a large army sitting in your house in the middle of war when you know they are equipped and trained to protect your country. You simply have to let them do what they do. Of course you want to protect your citizens from domestic issues. You want to protect your land so it does not turn into a chaotic mess. However, putting everyone at the same post isn't going to do much either. You diversify the stations and posts so that you are taken care of globally while decreasing blind spots.

The same is true for your savings.

Saving is best done when focused on specific usage with specific goals in mind—for example, saving to build an emergency fund or saving for down payment for a home. Saving and letting money sit in a bank account where interest is less than inflation is money being lost. If your money isn't growing past inflation, you are losing money.

PAYING ODE TO COMPOUNDING

Early in my financial journey, I had invested in a simple index fund (more on that later). I remember looking at my account balance in the middle of the year and being surprised by how much I had in there. It was a good year in general for the stock market and returns were at an all-time high. In the span of six months, my money had over a 20 percent return. It felt like someone had added more money while I was sleeping! My money was literally birthing more money! Considering that I hadn't taken additional calls or shifts to create this, my mind was blown!

This was when the impact of compounding interest really became clear. There are many ways to go from Los Angeles to NYC. You can walk or bike there. You can take the train and you can fly there. Walking will take you an estimated 914 hours. Biking is an estimated 253 hours. The fastest train ride would be about three days and flying is an average of six hours.

The length of time matters. Your condition at the time of arrival would also differ.

The same is true for money and financial goals. Without compounding, you may get there. With compounding, you have a better chance of getting there faster, healthier, and without overworking.

In essence, compounding interest refers to the concept in which money invested grows over time in a nonlinear fashion. It grows exponentially. If you buy an investment product and you get paid interest on that investment, the growth on your investment has a multiplier effect. You earn interest on your interest, which accelerates growth. That way, your money growth continues to get stronger over time. Your money makes you more money. The compounding frequency varies based on many factors such as specific vehicle, market, or economy and it can vary from daily to annually.

This is in contrast to simple interest in which the interest is only on the principal and typically calculated over a year as seen in personal loans, mortgages, and car loans.

The beauty of compounding interest is why you need to start investing today. The longer time your money spends "on the court," the more likely it is to grow. Investing as early as possible beats waiting to find "the perfect time" to invest. As physicians, many of us do not start investing until our thirties. This is in contrast to our colleagues who may have started investing right after college or shorter postgraduate programs. We definitely need to start now.

BARRIERS TO INVESTING

When I speak with physicians, every single person I speak to wants to invest. What is interesting is the mismatch between the interest in investing and actually investing. In order for us to effectively close some of the gaps and disparities that exist in investment, we have to understand some of the barriers. Here are some of the most common reasons women physicians don't invest.

I DON'T KNOW HOW

When Idris joined The MoneyFitMD Money School for badass women physicians, she was already a very successful physician. She had graduated at the top of her class and had matched into a very highly sought-after surgical subspecialty. She had now been in practice for almost a decade and amounted multiple six figures in savings. Thinking about the amount of cash she had sitting in a savings account was a point of embarrassment for her. "Latifat, I wish someone that I trust could show me how to invest." After going through the core curriculum that forms the foundation of our money curriculum, she was able to start investing. In the span of six months, she had maximized her work-related pretax retirement accounts and her post-tax Roth investment accounts. She also invested in her first real estate syndication and is currently working on investing in her first active investment. She told me, "I wish I had learned this earlier. I would have been investing a long time ago."

Many of us are not taught by our families. Maybe they also didn't know or they were victims in a world where talking about money is thought to be taboo and uncomfortable. This lack of knowledge may especially be the case if you are one of the first in your family to even conceive of building wealth. Maybe this wasn't something your parents or guardians even knew, let alone talked about.

It would be great if our parents taught us everything we needed to know about everything. Money was historically used as an object to promote sexism and racism. For many parents and generations before, they lived in a post-colonization world where white men were considered the gold standard. Your parents may be victims too. "Women shouldn't ask for too much; they should blend in the background." It's no surprise that most of the financial education geared toward women focuses more on saving and budgeting and not enough on investments. We are changing that.

Unfortunately, our medical education does not cover these foundations. Most medical students do not get the Money 101 or 102 talk in medical school. By the time we are attendings, it can be difficult to know where to look for educational materials without feeling like we are being swindled.

However, as resourceful women, we know how to unleash the

power of learning when we are interested. So maybe the reason you don't know is because you weren't taught. But now, going forward, the only reason you won't is because you are choosing to not learn. You can change that narrative today. Find a trusted guide or source and commit to learning and taking actions.

INVESTING LOOKS COMPLICATED

When I met Linda, she already had many investments. She has been investing in simple index funds and was automating the investments so that every month, on a specific day, she invested a specific predetermined amount of money to buy more funds. However, there was an unsettled thought that was repeatedly coming to her mind. "It cannot be this easy. There is a more complicated, more correct way to do this that I am missing." She was a mixture of reassured and surprised to find that simple investments can be successful overall and simple investments had more chances of success than actively managed accounts.

Once she realized this and confirmed that her investment style was a reflection of her goals and risk tolerance, she knew she was doing it right!

As physicians, we have been fed this crap that "complicated investments are better." But this is not true.

For one, if we are not accustomed to looking at the numbers; it may seem more complicated than it really is. However, as physicians, we learn all kinds of crazy stuff. We have memorized more things than many people will ever need to. We are masters at assessment and planning. Investing is not even close to being as complicated as being a physician. If you can learn medicine, you can learn investing.

Also, complicated isn't more likely to be successful than simple. Simple investments are excellent investments. Based on data, simple investing can be successful investing.

I DON'T KNOW WHO TO TRUST TO LEARN

When I began my financial journey, one of my first moves was to hire a financial advisor. I had not invested time into my own personal learning. I believed that if I could just find an expert who knows more about this, then I could mind my own business. What I didn't know was that as a physician, there was a tag on me that said, "She is too busy to care. She is too busy and overwhelmed to try." For this reason, my advisor was investing in ways that seemed to do more to pad their pockets than mine. It was after I began learning for myself and asking questions that I finally began to see that knowing who to trust is as important as knowing what to invest in. And learning and investing in my own education is key to building a well-trusted team. If you are not minding your money, you are not truly minding your business.

The more I equipped myself, the more I was able to effectively screen to ensure that decisions are made with my preferred outcome in mind. Yes, you have to do your due diligence; however, it is possible to find trusted sources of knowledge transfer.

Leverage your relationships. Ask for references or recommendations from people you trust to give unbiased information. On *The MoneyFitMD* podcast, you can find information on how to interview a prospective advisor if you choose to have one. You may also choose to hire a fee-only advisor with fiduciary duties. This means that they are legally bound to invest with your interests primarily. You would think this would be a requirement for all advisors, but unfortunately, it's not.

In the MoneyFitMD school, you will find many physicians investing successfully. Some are taking the DIY path while others are choosing to work with fee-only advisors with fiduciary responsibilities. The best way to screen is to empower yourself in knowledge. That way, you may choose to self-manage, but if not, at least your money will be in the hands of someone vetted by you.

I DON'T HAVE TIME; INVESTING TAKES TIME

After working an average of fifty hours per week, the last thing Daria wanted was to stare at her finances with ignorance. As an emergency medicine physician, she was busy. Therefore, it was easy for her to blame time as the reason why she wasn't taking care of her finances. She recently shared with me that "once I decided to focus on my finances, the interesting thing was, I found the time." We find time for things that matter most to us and what we focus on grows. What we ignore completely is less likely to grow.

Learning to invest takes as much or little time as you assign the task. Everything grows. Everything compounds, especially when given the right soil. Investing doesn't have to be active and held down. Learn the basics. Learn the power of automation. Keep it moving. The most important thing is to start. You can start by looking at what you are already invested in. Many physicians have a form of retirement account like a 401(k), 403(b), or similar. Take a look. How much are you paying in fees? These are referred to as expense ratios, and lower ratios are preferred to decrease loss in value of your investment through high fees.

During intern year, we spend an average of eighty hours learning. The transition from embodying being a medical student versus being an intern is impressive and we accomplish that feat by marinating in the space. The more time you spend immersed in money, the easier it suddenly feels. That time doesn't have to be at once; it can accumulate. The more you do it, the more doable it becomes. Imagine thinking medical school looked hard from the perspective of a college student and choosing not to start. The way to conquer is to get into it. We start by starting. There is no other way to master it.

BUT I HAVE AN ADVISOR

There is nothing wrong with having an advisor. An advisor with transparent fees can be a part of your team. Like any other expense, it's important to make sure they are giving you value for the cost paid. If you choose to have one, they are simply one of the components of a team of which you are the CEO. If you don't know the basics or foundation, how will you know if your investment is doing well or not? Compared to what?

One client of mine thought her investments were doing great. She was having an annual return of ~10 percent. That year, returns in the stock market were crazy high. Most people were having returns of ~20 percent and above. She assumed her returns were great until she learned otherwise. Another client had the intention of firing her advisor. Her goal was to equip herself to learn enough to take the reins. Once she became financially literate, she found out that he was doing great. She didn't need the advisor, but she chose to keep him as a part of her team. Let the data speak. Look at the numbers. They don't hurt. Making decisions from not knowing can burn you.

I'M NOT SURE WHERE TO START

Ellen is a physician. She's in her forties. She's very hardworking and excelled throughout medical school. She had been thinking of opening an investment account, but her fear about messing up was preventing any productive actions. Every time she considered doing something different than clinical medicine, she felt crippled by fear of failure. The thought of the fear was enough to keep her from taking the bold steps. She had to learn to allow the emotion.

As she worked on herself, her why became stronger than the desire to avoid the fear of the emotion. As she took actions, it became even easier to take more financial actions and make decisions. The ability to make decisions quickly without should-ing ourselves is one of the most important characteristics we need to develop if we want to increase our net worth. The more decisions you make, the more financially confident you will be.

I AM AFRAID OF MAKING MISTAKES

I hate making mistakes. As a teenager, it felt like the worst thing that could happen. I have memories about so many episodes of fresh tears over the pain and agony of making mistakes. I wish someone had relieved my young soul of that anguish and explained to me that mistakes aren't the opposite of success. A mistake is the path or doorway you have to get through in order to succeed.

As physicians, the stakes can feel higher. Mistakes clinically can lead to negative outcomes including loss of life for patients we care deeply about. Most of us carry the memories with us. Painfully so. What if the most painful part isn't the actual event but instead the belief or thought and expectation that this should not happen? What if we accepted that as much as we excel at everything to avoid it, it is like a battle scar of what creates an attending attendier.

The high stakes of mistakes in medicine can make it conceptually difficult for us to access the concept that mistakes can be part of your normal journey in money. Show me a person who has never made a financial mistake and I will show you someone who is not achieving their financial goals. Mistakes will happen. It is how we learn and grow. The key is to diversify your investments and not put all your eggs in one basket. That way, even if (or when) you do make financial mistakes or get less-than-ideal results, you have a buffer.

Unexpected outcomes will happen. Knowing you can always pivot is a true mark of a growth-centered mindset.

People say that knowledge is power. I say knowledge followed by action is power. You are staying disempowered when you don't take action due to an overwhelming fear of mistakes. The key is to change your thoughts about it. You are badass enough to diversify and grow no matter what.

George Foreman is a well-known former heavyweight boxer. He won the heavyweight championship in 1973. He retired from boxing and became an ordained minister. He filed for bankruptcy in 1983. Down and out, with no other options available, he returned to boxing for financial reasons. In 1994, he became the oldest heavyweight champion. He also began doing ads, speaking, and product endorsements. In 1994, he came up with the idea of the Foreman Grill. In 1999, he sold the rights for $130 million.

Failure, even when it happens, doesn't ever have to be the end unless you say so!

HOW TO GET STARTED

For what it's worth, I want to remind you that based on data, women are less likely to invest. However, when we do, we are more likely to actually do well.[7] So next time your brain screams and says you are going to mess it up, just remind yourself that everything is figureoutable and you've got this.

In order to best decide the right investment vehicle for you, here are some guides that are key to know.

YOUR GOALS AND TIMELINE

When do you expect to need the money that you are investing and the returns? Your timeline will determine how aggressively you invest. Are you needing your investments to fund your life currently or are you intending them for it to be for use decades from now? The benefit of clarifying this is that it will help you decide how important cash flow or short-term returns are to you or if focusing on long-term returns is the primary outcome.

---

7   Maurie Backman, "Women and Investing: 20 Years of Research and Statistics Summarized," The Motley Fool, last updated March 9, 2022, https://www.fool.com/research/women-in-investing-research/.

If you need the money in the next three to five years, you may choose to invest in a less volatile and more "conservative" vehicle such as a high-interest savings account, government bonds, or money market accounts. The returns from these investments will vary based on the economy; however, in general, they tend to be less volatile.

Although investing in stocks (even if diversified) may boost your chances of a better return, it may be riskier since no one knows for certain what the stock market will be doing. No one could have anticipated the recent global pandemic.

RISK TOLERANCE

Each person will have a varying risk tolerance. There is no one size fits all. Remember, the point of doing money is so that you can sleep well at night without worrying about money. Therefore, your investment strategy has to foster your ability to sleep well at night now and in future. It is important to not exaggerate or assume your own risk tolerance. Major investment platforms such as Vanguard provide free investment risk tolerance quizzes to give you an idea of your risk tolerance and suggestions on your aggressive and conservative investment strategies. If you plan to retire within five years, I highly recommend consulting with a well-vetted, fee-only-based fiduciary financial advisor to guide your investment and withdrawing strategy.

Developing your proficiency in a non-fear-based approach is essential to helping stay the course and avoiding FOMO (fear of missing out)-based investing. "Because everyone is doing it" is the worst reason to invest. It is no surprise that when we are in the middle of a catastrophe, we are more likely to make erratic decisions. Therefore, the best time to make decisions about investment strategies is *not* in the middle of the chaos. Make important decisions when you are thinking clearly. When emotions are high or fear is in action, stay away from making significant changes in your decisions. Decide on a plan. Stay with it.

REST STOP: YOUR GOALS MATTER

1. Where do you want to be financially in three years?

2. Where do you want to be financially in five years?

3. What dreams do you currently have? By when do you want to have these manifest?

4. Write it down. The eyes can't see what the mind cannot. Goals that are written down are more likely to be created.

Your investment vehicles will be personal based on your age, risk tolerance, social convictions, and personal goals. A thirty-seven-year-old physician who has no plans of using her investment or returns to support her current living is more likely to invest more aggressively for a chance of higher returns than Angie, who is closer to retiring.

WAYS TO INVEST

In general, investing can be done through the following:

1. **Ownership:** This may be as part owner of a company through owning stocks in the company, real estate investment trusts (REITs), real estate funds, syndications or other real estate partnerships, or being an equity partner in a company or

actual product. It may also be through you directly owning the company such as owning your private practice, franchise, or business ventures.

2. **Debt investing:** This may be by you functioning as the bank by offering loans to individuals or businesses in return for interest. These can be seen in real estate contracts, hard money lending, student loan lending, and private equity. These may be higher risk in general with a chance of higher return. Such risks need to be weighed in context of your entire portfolio. Debt investing can also be through providing debt to large corporations through bonds or government securities.

For a simple guide to investing, I highly recommend *The Boglehead Guide to Investing* by John Bogle and *The Coffeehouse Investor* by Bill Schultheis. Don't be stuck in perfectionism or inaction due to fear.

What about real estate? Most of the wealthiest people invest in real estate. Success always leaves clues. Real estate is one of the most tax-efficient ways to build wealth. Physicians are positioned to excel as real estate investors.

To ensure that you are positioning yourself to invest well in real estate, here are three things I recommend:

1. **Do your due diligence:** To ensure that your investment is truly an asset and not a liability, it is important to invest in good-quality investments. The details of this are beyond the scope we are covering here. However, in order to invest well and acquire assets rather than liabilities, it is important to know how to screen properties for goods deals versus bad deals. Depending

on your investment goal and market, I typically recommend purchasing properties that have cash flow. This means investing in properties that cover your expenses and leave you a return on your investment. Although this may be difficult in cities with a high cost of living, it is important to know that you can live where you want but to invest where the numbers and return makes sense. Buying a property simply because someone is willing to sell to you is a decision that may backfire. Learn what defines a good deal. On our weekly podcast, *The MoneyFitMD*, we interview physicians and guests investing in various sectors of the economy including real estate.

2. **Leverage your community:** You are the average of the five to six people you surround yourself with. Your community sets the temperature of your room. One of the most important decisions I made in my money journey was to come into rooms of people I aspire to be. It is important to be able to access individuals or organizations whose value may be in line with what you want the world to be like. For that reason, I invest a lot personally to have access to such communities so that I can continue to provide access and quality to my own community for women physicians. A great community will bridge you and connect you to possible investors with whom you can partner.

3. **Invest in your learning process:** For years, I had wanted to invest in real estate. I had looked at free content online but never took the plunge. Three years ago, I decided to invest in a real estate coaching program. Within a year, I bought ten rental doors. As women physicians, our time is of value. Investing in the learning process can help shorten the time it takes to reach your goals.

There is a myth that real estate is hard. As with everything else, myths are meant to derail the uncommitted, the skeptic, and the majority. As physicians, there is no one more suited to accomplish hard things. In my experience, it is easier than I expected. The important thing is to learn the tools and persist.

Another myth is that you need to have a lot of time to invest. Mira had always been interested in real estate. However, between a busy practice and a growing family, she was having difficulty finding the time to start. When she joined our private money community for women physicians, we helped her clarify her goals. Her goal was to have cash flow from real estate investment as well as enjoy some of the tax benefits that are legally available for investors. Four months after joining, she decided that syndications were a better fit for her in this season. She is now invested in her first real estate syndication and looking forward to investing in her next.

Real estate investing can be actively done by buying a property and then either self-managing or hiring a property manager. However, other options exist. Syndications are partnerships in which a sponsor congregates money from different sources to invest in a specific building. This can be a great option for busy physicians who may be unable to devote the time. Alternatively, you can invest in funds. These are also collections of investors putting their money together with the purpose of investing in different projects.

The key is to ensure appropriate vetting of the potential partnerships.

There are other investment vehicles such as gold, cryptocurrency, and cash. The key is to have this as a small percentage of your portfolio in general due to volatility while keeping more classic investments as the majority of your investments.

The way to demystify wealth is to dig deeper and ask the right questions. We can learn from our communities. How are they doing it? Is it possible that you can learn to invest in a way that's in line with your value? Is it possible to grow wealth consciously and ethically? Maybe it is. Maybe it's possible to learn. Maybe it's possible to escape the rat race. Maybe.

It is possible.

You are a badass physician after all.

RX SUMMARY

1. Compound interest is described as the eighth wonder of the world. Use it.

2. Decide on an investment plan based on your risk tolerance and goals.

3. Simple investing can be excellent investing.

CHAPTER 7

Ditch Hustle, Build Riches

Shayna was exhausted. As a hardworking emergency medicine physician, she is no stranger to working hard. She recently celebrated her tenth year in practice and she was starting to feel the burn. Swinging between day and night shifts while also trying to balance life as a single mom of three children was no easy feat. Her plan was to cut down her clinical hours, but between childcare cost and paying off her student loans, there didn't seem to be too much wiggle room. A few years prior, she had joined a network marketing team as a way of starting a side gig. After a few months, she terminated because it just seemed she barely had any wiggle room to breathe. She was worn-out and still struggling financially. During one of our conversations, she mumbled, "I am just tired of overworking at everything. I really don't want to keep hustling like this. I am tired."

Does this sound familiar?

After years and years of eighty-hour work weeks to get through medical school, we have been conditioned to believe that having money means working and hustling harder. We believe that the only way to earn more is to spend more living hours hustling. This belief has caused more frustration and angst for the average physician.

But you are not average.

As physicians, we have a long list of to-dos. Between seeing patients, charting, reviewing labs, returning calls, and in baskets, the days are spent. It may seem accurate to think that the more hours we spend working, the more we should be earning.

What if this thought is affecting your financial growth adversely?

Let's unpack.

Consider this scenario. You charge per hour. There is a limit to how much you can fit into twenty-four hours. Most of us don't work twenty-four hours per day every single day. So there's a limit to how much you would be able to earn since your hours are finite.

When you are thinking in a hustling kind of way, you think tacking additional money-generating activities to the end of your already long day is the only way to grow your money.

Hustling mindset is an energetic space that comes from a wandering mindset, lack of belief in your own resourcefulness, and a whole layer of FOMO (fear of missing out), based on scarcity. It feels hard. It feels stressful. It depletes instead of nourishes. It is restless and ignores the yearnings and needs of the body. It is that unsettling feeling you have when "there is something else that *should* be done" because you have accepted the cultural standard that there is simply only one way to do great—the hustle way. This is different from the act of working diligently on a specific singular course of action until you create the result you want. Hustling in the form of doing what it takes to get to a singular result is different from a hustling mindset that is restless.

When you are confident in your long-term goals, you hustle less. When you know that no amount of money will replace a low self-concept or poor relationship with yourself, you hustle less. When you believe that you have an abundant source with your name on it, you hustle less. You create a plan from a grounded space and you quiet the voices that come up to tell you "It will never be enough" or "You are not financially secure yet."

It's already enough.

You are already enough.

DIVERSIFY, NOT DIE-VERSIFY

Rebecca has been in clinical practice for twenty-five years. After much procrastination, she was ready to get started in her real estate journey. She chose to invest in Las Vegas. At first glance, it seemed like there were no deals to be found. She had been looking on the real estate marketing sites and was not finding anything that fit her criteria. She chose to explore other locations and ended up in another state. At first look, it seemed there weren't great deals there either. She was again ready to move on. But this time, she decided to give it more time and dig deeper. By focusing and digging more deeply, she was able to find great deals. She chose to focus and look "like a pathologist."

As a gastroenterologist, I value the input of my pathology colleagues. When reviewing slides with them, I am always amazed by their systematic and detailed approach used in reviewing. They start by zooming out and then zooming in. They bring the slide into focus using the knobs on their microscope. They slide it around, looking in sections to find what an untrained eye and mind cannot see. I call this the pathology way to investing. You focus by starting wide and then narrowing into the depths. This works when you are looking for investment deals. It worked for Rebecca.

It is important to not simply invest broadly but also deeply. This will bring you the power of focus. The power of constraint. It can be done.

What is die-versify? This is a term I use to describe the phenomenon in which people think they have to invest in everything in order to feel successful. It's from the thought of "not enough." It is based on an energy of hustling. Most cases of this will require overstretching in terms of the number of investing buckets. Die-versifying is putting money and investments in each type of investment. You will know you are die-versified if your investments are so stretched out that there's only a little in too many buckets. This is also accompanied by unsettling, unrest, darting eye movements looking for "any" next best thing.

There is no rest. No peace. Never enough.

Picture a cell phone trying to find internet reception in a baseline. The continued act of looking and trying to establish connection can deplete its battery at an accelerated rate. That phone may die faster too. That can happen to us too.

This is not where you want to be. Yes, diversify. Yes, learn. Yes, grow. But don't die-versify.

Invest in multiple streams, yes. Make sure each stream is solid enough to make the return tangible.

How many sources of income do you need? Many financial platforms will say seven. I saw as many as you want to achieve your goal without the wonky instability, grinding, or FOMO energy. What do I mean by that?

You only have to be online for five seconds before you hear about another "best, quickest source of income that will get you to millionaire status." Crypto? Options? Individual stocks? There is nothing wrong with any of these. However, it is critically important to guard your money brain.

GUARD YOUR MONEY BRAIN

It is important to make decisions, decide your path, and silence the noise. For most physicians starting out, it may seem like the options for investing are limited. However, as you continue this journey and implement the strategies we have covered so far, you will start to see that there are many options. There is a new idea springing forth every week or month. It is important to ensure that you have your strategies and stay your course. Your money brain is not a front porch for anyone to walk on. Be intentional about who you let into that space. It is a sacred space that you have to guard, otherwise you will spend time and energy chasing shiny options only to end up depleted and overwhelmed. Your time and energy are your most valued assets.

Choose your vehicles of wealth and money generation. Plan them, tend them, let them grow. Then once they look like they can stand without you tending to them by the second, you can diversify to others. This may mean automating the systems, building systems, or hiring team members to delegate to.

Be intentional that your investment combines both active and passive options. Invest enough to not dilute out the gains to the point that it's of no value. Avoid FOMO energy. There will always be a new thing. Let the core be core.

Yes, have fun and explore, but let that be from a place of groundedness, not shakiness or FOMO energy. There are many ways to skin a cat. What matters most is setting your money goals, setting how to achieve them, and welcoming new ideas, but never at the expense of your wellness or peace of mind.

TIME, THE MOST VALUABLE ASSET

A few years ago, I realized I was packing more into my twenty-four hours than many others. I was working pretty much full time as a physician. My husband and I had young children. We led a Bible study group. We were investing in real estate and actively looking for properties. At that time, I had also started MoneyFitMD and had not mastered the act of delegation to my team yet. I had multiple sources of income. My schedule was packed to the second. If it was not on my calendar, it wasn't getting done. I was not giving myself space between commitments. I was exhausted. The idea or thought of adding on anything else seemed like an overkill.

This is true for most physicians. This is why it is critical to dissociate time and money.

Creating multiple sources of income doesn't have to mean creating multiple jobs. It is essential to leverage your money so that it can work for you. A stream may be through the stock market by buying assets passively or passive real estate investment through real estate investment trusts (REITs), syndications, or other publicly available mechanisms. Another source of income can be through affiliate marketing, blogging, product development, well automated online selling through electronic commerce (product selling on Amazon is a popular option), course development where you teach one to many, alternative investments through hard money lending, investments in farmlands, and other opportunities. The most important thing is to decide, do due diligence, and take action.

As you go forward and build your multiple sources of income, it's important to ensure that you complement the various kinds or categories of income.

ACTIVE VERSUS PASSIVE

Whether something is active or passive means is a way to assess how actively involved you are in the day-to-day running of operations. If you are spending hours per week or month on the management or income source, then it can be considered active. Passive, on the other hand, refers to the minimal time involvement needed directly from you after the initial setting up or vetting process.

For instance, say I buy a property that I am renting out. If I am managing it myself, it would be considered active. However, if I have a great property manager who takes care of the day-to-day running, then it may be more passive.

EMPLOYEE INCOME VERSUS BUSINESS OWNER INCOME

As physicians, we work hard for our clinical income. Considering the high rate of burnout and overwork that currently exists in our culture, it is important to diversify and create a level of time autonomy. It is harder to create that autonomy as an employee. Employee income is also typically in the highest tax category. The tax code is written to favor business owners and real estate investors. In order to optimize your finances and be tax efficient, it is important to broaden your income into the ownership category.

SHORT TERM VERSUS MEDIUM TERM VERSUS LONG TERM

The definition of the specific amount of time will depend on your unique situation. Short term typically refers to income you want to use in the next twelve months. Medium term may represent income you don't need access to now and can wait two to ten years. Long term will refer to money you need access to after that.

Combining these various sources will help you grow your net worth while decreasing overworking. It will also help with tax optimization. Be sure to employ the help of a forward-thinking tax professional.

WHAT ABOUT SIDE GIGS?

I had no idea side gigs were a thing until near the end of my fellowship training. As a busy physician, the last thing I needed was another thing on the side. As discussed earlier, I assumed my sole physician income was dependable enough to be financially secure.

Side gigs have gotten increasingly popular in the physician community. It's a good thing. However, the term "side gig" suggests a minor, after-hour, low-income potential to it. It is important to bring abundance into the idea of what you are creating. You are building an income source in its own right.

Think goal focused, not time focused. If your goal is to create $20,000 per year, that's the goal. The time allotment isn't what's key. If you call it a side gig, it has a higher chance of staying small. If you think of it as a bona fide business, it has a better potential to become something more complete that deserves its own life.

It's a mentality shift. Our language truly does matter.

There are financial and nonfinancial benefits to creating alternative sources of income.

First, the direct financial benefit as an income source.

Second, the indirect financial benefit for tax planning purposes. Creating additional nonemployment-based income sources can allow you to have more options for retirement investments. Real estate can be a great tax-efficient vehicle. IRS-permitted business-related expenses can also provide tax optimization and improve life experiences. For instance, attending a business-related conference can also double benefit as part vacation. There are rules on how you can do this in an IRS-compliant way. Your CPA or tax planner can provide more specific information to guide you.

There are nonfinancial benefits as well.

As physicians, daily practice of medicine can become routine when done day in and day out. This can lead to boredom, which, combined with other factors, can accelerate burnout. Using a different part of your analytic brain can provide mental respite from the regular.

For many physicians, clinical income is the predominant source of our income. The lack of sufficient financial education in our training and high student debt burden can contribute to a state of feeling stuck, a state of thinking we have no options but to maintain the status quo. Having alternative sources of income can be an active lifeline reminding you of resourcefulness.

THE TRUTH ABOUT PASSIVE INCOME

Imagine if you let your money work for you, meaning you invest passively. This means making an income even when you are not physically giving the value that's creating the money in that moment, thereby decreasing overwork and increasing the freedom of time.

First, let's define passive income. Passive income refers to income from sources that don't require a one-to-one exchange of money to time after the initial establishment phase.

What do I mean by that? Anything you choose to invest in will need a setup phase. The best analogy is medical treatments that require a loading and maintenance phase.

In order to invest, even passively, you have to do your due diligence. You want to investigate who you are partnering with, look at their financial books or statements as well as history to ensure it's the right fit for you in terms of projected return, ethics surrounding the kind of investment, the projected timeline of return, and anticipated risk level. This may sound overwhelming for a new investor. However, this information can be obtained through educational content and webinars provided by sponsors. This is also the importance of being in communities where referrals and recommendations can be made. In The MoneyFitMD community, the goal is for women physicians to take control of their finances without overworking. We bring in investors who educate our members and notify them of possible options for investing. Although these also have to be analyzed and vetted and no single investor is guaranteed, it provides a cozier and less overwhelming environment to obtain the information needed.

The term "passive income" may be misinterpreted to mean complete hands off, but this is a misnomer. Most investments may feel more active during induction but expected to be more passive during maintenance.

Expectation is key. Don't let the initial phase discourage you. Dividend-producing stock market investments can be a form of passive income, as can investment in projects such as farming, coffee plantations, REITS, e-commerce, hard money lending, crowdsourcing, and equity partnership in business ownership.

Building in passive income sources is going to be important as you scale and grow your finances. It frees you up to pursue work you are passionate about without letting money or time be a limiting factor.

RX SUMMARY

1. Time is your biggest asset.

2. Earning and having more doesn't mean hustling. You can achieve in a way that nourishes your soul.

3. Diversify your income source in a way that honors your time, needs, and goals.

CHAPTER 8

The New Generational Wealth

As women physicians, we spent our twenties and thirties training to be excellent at what we do. We do that because we care about our communities and want to create positive changes. When we have money, we do good in the world. Our contributions should not come at the expense of our health and wellness and they cannot come from an empty vessel. We have to learn to receive so we can give even bigger. If you subconsciously continue to avoid wealth because you think it is immoral, nothing will change.

As women physicians, passing financial legacies are at the forefront of our minds. Even for those without children, bringing finances into our families is oftentimes at the front of our minds.

How are we going to take our place at the tables where these important conversations are happening? We are the secret sauce. We already know what the world looks like without us claiming our money space. It's time for a different experiment.

Now imagine a future when you can fuel your passion project. When being rich is equivalent and synonymous to being good. When spending is not something to be ashamed of but becomes the catalyst for exercising your true value.

Imagine a future where our youth knew they were enough. Period. Not based on the size of their pocket or what they do but simply who they are. My opinion is that the moment we are born, we are at maximum capacity of our value. It doesn't diminish. If we choose to be physicians or stay-at-home parents or politicians or technicians, our value as humans is still at its peak simply because we are beautifully and wonderfully made in all diverse forms, shades, and shapes.

When we learn these foundations for ourselves and we see it, do it, and teach it, it becomes a catalyst that will change family trees.

Generational wealth isn't simply about cash.

Passing on the foundations of money and wealth is so key. When we redefine wealth, we redefine purpose and redefine communities.

USE YOUR WEALTH FOR GOOD

Karen grew up with a single mom. She has memories of her mom working many jobs to take care of her and her siblings. When she had the opportunity to learn about real estate investing, she had an unconscious visceral reaction to the idea of collecting rent. "Am I going to be contributing to the financial stress of families? Am I going to be one of 'those rich people'? Am I going to be part of the problem?"

Here was my question to her:

Have you ever seen something that pissed you off so much, yet you know it was backed by someone's money?

How does staying out of the game help? Your experience makes you the exact best person to have these tools in their hands. When people of various backgrounds and experiences come to the table and learn how to build wealth consciously, we are truly redefining wealth—not only for women physicians but for the world. We preserve communities and augment them.

As a landlord, I have had the privilege of being a part of the change I want to see. We once walked into an apartment infested with mold. It had previously been owned by a landlord who hadn't fixed this issue that existed for years. This particular unit was inhabited by a family with four children. As a physician, I know the health effects of this. We fixed the mold problem urgently.

They pay rent. We provide excellent value in a way that allows us to sleep great at night. The investment has to be an asset, not a liability. Liabilities will burn you out and prevent you from doing good for the long haul. If it's a liability, I may have to sell it. How does that help? Our tenants like having us as landlords. Not because we are offering free housing, but because we are giving remarkable value at fair market price while maintaining the community.

The goal isn't for you to think I have it perfected. We always aim for better. The point is to reinforce to you that the hand that holds the knife is key.

ETHICAL GIVING/PHILANTHROPY

In 2022, I was at a mastermind event in Austin. Many of the attendees were people I had met previously. This was at the beginning of the Russian attack on Ukraine. One of my mentors, Simone Seol of Joyful Marketing, mentioned that she wanted to use this as a way of raising funds to support medical missions for local hospitals in Ukraine.

This is how we use our voice and position for impact.

How can you bring more consciousness into wealth building?

How can you build assets in a way that builds health and wellness for you and members of your community?

Where are you investing currently?

Where is your money going currently? Are you happy with where your money is going? Is it in line with your values?

If you believe in climate change, are your stock investments reflecting that?

If you do not believe in privatization of the prison systems, is your investment reflective of that?

Not investing at all is not the solution. Increasing your awareness is. Then, when we know better, we do better. Invest differently. Build wealth. Take up space at the table.

Money provides economic power. I cannot think of better people to guide that power than women physicians.

Giving is not a destination. It's a process. It's not a light at the end of the tunnel. It is now. If you think it's easier to give when you have more money, you may be in for a surprise. Giving is as much of a gift to the giver as it is to the receiver.

If you are finding it hard to give, it may be related to a socialization that spending is bad. It may be because you think you don't have enough to give. The key is to start by starting. If you find it hard to give $200 because it feels uncomfortable, do you think it will feel more comfortable to give $20,000?

Start building your giving muscle now but not at the expense of your growth. We can build wealth *and* give; it doesn't have to be either/or.

Money is neutral.

Wealth is neutral.

Money in your hands means money in your community. When you stay out of the game intentionally or out of fear, you are contributing to the issue and keeping the status quo. We already know what the world looks like without your optimal money magic. Let's try another experiment with you as the magic source.

BUILDING YOUR FINANCIAL LEGACY

Kate grew up in a middle-class Black family. Growing up, she was very aware of the impact of racism on wealth. She saw it in the differences in the quality of schools in her neighborhood compared to those in the schools she was bused to miles away in the same city. When she was in medical school, her parents lost their home. She still remembers how difficult that was for them. Her dad worked in the city system in transportation. Her mom worked at a mosque. For her, wealth wasn't even something she remotely considered. The privilege of a physician income was the ultimate dream. As she learned the information you have learned so far in this book, she began to dig herself out from the cycle of paycheck-to-paycheck living. She paid off her student debt. She realized that being rich was something that was actually possible for someone like her.

Since then, she has gone on to teach her parents these same foundations. For the first time in her adult life, her parents have no more credit card debt. She now sponsors scholarships to promote health and sciences at those same schools she was bused from.

Financial legacy is in part about passing cash to our descendants. However, the cash is just a fragment of that. When you build wealth, it changes family trees, makes it even more possible for the next generation, and has the potential to change the world.

The numeric part of money is simple and can be learned in a day. The core, the character, the mentality—that is the real generational wealth. When we learn how to change how we think, when we learn how to sharpen our millionaire brains, we can learn how to fish in any freaking water.

I am often asked how to teach kids about money. As parents and guardians, we want them set so we can build wealth for generations.

Learn what is in this book. Have conversations about it at the dinner table, in the car. Point out examples of how money is good and a tool for change, not to be hoarded, not to be handled with guilt, not to be treated as a hot potato. But like energy that is channeled through all of us, so it can reach more sources.

Teach children about the power of compounding. Teach them to invest in their future in a way that would make their eighty-year-old version proud without sacrificing the needs of their current self. We call this paying themselves first, before liabilities are purchased. Also teach them how to be physically, mentally, and mindfully well in a way that is not scarcity based.

Teach kids to work hard and work smart, to think about both active and passive wealth. To give, receive, and solve problems. Let's spend less time asking who they want to be and spend more time asking what they want to add to the world. Teach them to be empowered in their ability to see problems, assess, and fix them.

Many parents will teach their kids about money from a place of fear and anxiety. Remember that they learn probably more from what we do not say than from what we say.

Last, you are never going to get it perfectly right. It's always progress over perfection.

What are you doing right?

What do you want to see created?

How can you bridge that gap?

We need your intelligence, your dollars, your morals, your ethics, and your purpose. All of that.

It's going to take all hands on deck.

Consider this a call to action.

You've got this.

RX SUMMARY

1. Use your wealth for good. Invest ethically and give generously.

2. Build your financial legacy by investing in your community and teaching your children about money.

CHAPTER 9

Curate Your Rich Life

As a woman physician, you may have thought your future was laid out for you. College, medical school, residency, maybe fellowship, get an employee physician job and stay there forever, retire at age sixty-five. And then we thank you for your service. Hopefully, you have the longevity and health to live and "enjoy the fruit of your labor."

There is nothing wrong with that path *if* that's what you want.

If you are reading this book, you probably want more. You know you are meant for more. You are not one for a "mass production" kind of life.

You have a choice in how you spend your time and how you spend your life. Maybe it hasn't always felt like that. Maybe it always seems like someone else is making the decisions and someone else has been in the driver's seat.

This is the point of a money revolution. It is to help you see that you don't have to follow some arbitrarily set-out path.

It's time to curate that rich life.

It's not your money *or* your life. It's your money *and* your life. You get to curate it.

Thinking you have no choice is a choice. You can decide what you want your clinical practice to look like. When your income is from diversified sources, you put less stress on your clinical work. You get to practice on your terms. You get to decide how many days you want to work or not. When you practice medicine in a way that's healthy and breathable, your patients ultimately win. You win. Your family wins.

When you really understand that you are already enough no matter what, you have less pressure to try and earn your worth or value. You learn to be. You show up authentically. You lead differently. Your voice becomes stronger and clearer. You become a force of impact. That is what the world of medicine needs.

As a badass woman physician, your genius exists in your space of true richness and liberation. You start to create from a place of abundance, growth, contribution because none of it defines who you are.

The number of hours you practice is a choice. Consider that. Your brain may give you so many reasons why that choice doesn't exist. But believing your brain is a choice. Whether you think you can or whether you think you can't, you are correct.

So what do you want your ideal life to be?

You get to create it. You have permission to dream again.

If all those external voices didn't exist, how would you live your life? It's time to create that.

If socialization, rules made by systems of oppression, patriarchy, and racism aren't the loudest voices in your head, what would you choose?

"It's going to take a lot of money" is a myth. I want you to question it. It's as simple as looking at how much you are earning and how much you need to make from alternative sources to replace all or part of that income.

Traditionally, medicine and society says work like crazy and then retire at age sixty-five. If you could talk to your future self, what do you think she would say in all her wisdom? What decisions or changes would your future self be glad you made?

As you answer these questions, the vision of your life will become clear.

Speaking for myself, doing this exercise is what led to this book. It led to my current clinical hours. It has created some dreams that are yet to be realized, but I will do so, because if I can dream it, I can achieve it.

Take some time and write down the answer to this exercise. Write that vision plan. Don't skip this.

CREATING TIME BY DELEGATION

If you learn anything from this book, here is one lesson you need to hold on to: delegate.

You cannot do it alone, and even if you could, I wouldn't want that for you. As women physicians, we have been conditioned to overwork. We seem to equate our value as what we do and how much we give. We forget that delegating is a superpower that can save lives. As the CEO of your financial life, you are the heart of your money. If you have been avoiding it, now is the time to take charge. When you lead, great things happen.

There are times when DIY makes sense, but there are other times when DIY will cost you. As you build wealth, it is important to have your team. Who becomes a part of your team will depend on what stage you are at in your journey. As women physicians of diverse backgrounds and money stories, you may have been taught to hoard the money by doing it all yourself.

This may be costing you in time and numbers.

The goal is to build wealth without burnout. Keep in mind that regardless of who you hire as part of your team, you are still the CEO. As we discussed earlier in this book, getting value in exchange for money spent is key and will guide you objectively in terms of when it's time to keep a member of your team and when it's time to let them go.

Having a team can not only help you build wealth but also work with you to curate your best life as that wealth compounds. Here are some members who may be part of your team.

TAX ADVISOR/CPA

Filing taxes only is not financial planning. Filing your taxes is the absolute minimum. You can use an online-based system like TurboTax, but as your wealth building starts to occur and as you start to build into business ownership and/or real estate, you may need to consult an expert. Tax planning is not a passive, retrospective act. It is an active, futuristic planning. A great tax strategist is worth their weight in gold.

LAWYER

When it comes to businesses and business structure, some of this can be DIY. However, it is important to secure the assistance of a lawyer for estate planning and complex business structure planning, which can vary state to state. Be sure to employ a lawyer who is confident in your local and state laws. Other scenarios where you may need specialized legal assistance include trademarking, protecting your interests and assets as you develop partnerships and other financial relationships, and local county or state-specific tenant and landlord laws. Don't be penny wise, pound foolish. You may not need a lawyer on retainer but having names of who would be in your corner will provide you with some confidence and peace of mind as you grow.

FINANCIAL ADVISOR

I get many questions about this one. You do not need a financial advisor. In fact, if you think you need a financial advisor, it means it's time to uplevel your financial education. You can want a financial advisor and a great financial advisor can be a valuable member of your team, but they do not replace your knowledge.

In fact, the more knowledgeable you are about the foundations of money, the more likely you are to optimize your advisor appropriately. As with any other expenses, ensure you are getting value in exchange for the money you are paying. It is also critical to know how your advisor is getting paid. Transparency is an important attribute and avoidance or lack of clarity is a red flag. Here are some questions that may be helpful to have clarified:

1. Are they getting paid a flat fee per year or a percentage of the assets under their management?

2. Are they managing your investments or are they advising only?

3. Are they making commissions based on what you are investing in? Once you are clear about the fees you are paying and the value you are getting, you can objectively decide if it's worth the investment in them as a part of your team.

4. Are they vehemently recommending buying investment vehicles that may not be of primary value to you? Whole life versus term life insurance comes up frequently. For the majority of physicians, term life is sufficient. If your investment vehicles are not optimized yet or if you are not yet in the financial space to have disposable income and your advisor is recommending anything but term life insurance, that may be a red flag.

Getting comfortable asking questions with curiosity will get you ahead and will help you gather the information you need for your litmus test.

MONEY COACH

A money coach is a professional whose job is to help empower you. A coach is not a financial advisor. I am a certified life coach, which allows me to help you identify the blocks standing in your way between your current money state and where you want it to be. A coach's job is to help you be better so you can achieve your goals faster and in a healthier manner.

Most industries and leaders have coaches. A speaking coach can help you become a better speaker so you can start speaking more confidently and shorten time from the present to appropriate speaking income generation. A singing coach can do the same for a singer. There are acting coaches and leadership coaches. Most CEOs of the largest companies have coaches. A money coach can help you with the equivalent of your finances.

COMMUNITY

This is important. As we empower women physicians, it is essential to build your community. You may have grown up in a place where money wasn't talked about or the principles of money are different from what you are trying to input and build into your future. Money remains a taboo topic in medicine. How can we earn it when we don't talk about it? How can we invest or negotiate better when we still feel shame and judgment about what we are doing or not doing? If we surround ourselves with people with similar lived experiences who understand where we are coming from, we can identify and neutralize some of our money-limiting thoughts or habits and help us build together.

I needed that supportive and like-minded community when I started my money journey. Unfortunately, it was lacking. So I created one for myself and women like me. Women with heart, women who may have been socialized to give and not receive. Women who are smart, kind, and simply want to learn money without shame, guilt, and splaining.

Creating this community and being a coach and guide has been one of the biggest honors of my life. Witnessing the financial transformation and confidence in these women is a gift. I believe medicine is better when women physicians have money. Day in and day out, these women are the evidence of this truth. We are creating a world where physicians' net worth in the multiple six figure and seven figure is the norm, the baseline. We will work in settings that are in line with our values, where our excellence is valued. We will work because we want to, not because we have to. The MoneyFitMD Money School for badass women physicians has become that community. Be sure to visit us at www.moneyfitmd.com/msb to learn how you can join this growing community of women physicians who are money badasses.

CREATE YOUR AUTOMATED LIFE

What do I mean by that? Of course we want to fully experience the parts of life that we want to enjoy and live. How about the other parts? Let's automate them.

First, you go through the list of what you want to create. How do you want to earn, give, and build? Go ahead and automate it.

Which bills need to be automated?

What gifts need automation?

What about investment?

What about vacations? Booking and deciding a year in advance?

Massage?

Date night?

Childcare or babysitter automated on standby monthly or weekly?

Learning to automate is so key to building your rich life. What do you need to help run your life more smoothly? Automation will make it happen without waiting for you to get to that one more thing on your to-do list.

Then, as the CEO, you get to review episodically.

RICH LIVES IN ACTION

Creating your own definition of a rich life and practicing in a way that's in line with your wellness doesn't take time or lots of money. Nor is it only available to those born into wealth. If we choose to think that, we are contributing to disparities.

Pick your life. Pick your recipe and get cooking.

Mary is a primary care physician. She knew she wanted to spend more time doing things that gave her joy. She loves clinical medicine but knew that to practice for the long haul, she needed self-care. She negotiated her hours at work. She was able to cut down by a day a week. She still saw the same number of patients and her income didn't decrease. For her, this created the space she needed to be well. She is able to take her children to school and get her personal time on Fridays. She enjoys solo day trips to visit some of her favorite local spots.

Jane is an intensivist. For her, practicing medicine means working four twelve-hour shifts per week. She loves taking care of her patients, but with the stress of the pandemic, she feels herself burning out. In her words: "I need to get my foot off the accelerator for a minute. I will be back." For her, taking her foot off the accelerator meant finding ways to supplement her income so she could take care of her mental health. She learned how to invest in real estate. She started investing in short-term and long-term rentals. She is making additional income that has made it easier to take the time she needed.

Kyle messaged me somewhat frantically on a Sunday. She was about to spend a lot of money on a van—an RV minivan to be specific. She hadn't paid off her student loans. She was in year three of a clinical job she was enjoying. Why buy a mini RV when she had debt she hadn't paid off?

I asked her a simple question:

Six months from now, will you be glad you bought the van, or will you wish you had the money back? Her answer was clear. Almost two years later, she has taken more trips with her family and done more local RV camping than she remembers over the last ten years of her career.

She's living her rich life. Her secondhand RV enhanced her rich life!

Your definition of rich may be different, but it is possible. The one question you need to ask is not "Why?" It's "How?" *How* can I? Dream again. You get to curate your own life.

Conclusion

I've never been a good swimmer. I wasn't taught to be a swimmer when I was little and I've tried multiple times. But I love water and being at the ocean so much that my husband says that I am the daughter of water, because it gives me so much joy and fulfillment. It's my place, but I didn't know how to swim.

I've tried learning. I've taken many classes. In fact, when I was a college student at the University of California, Los Angeles (UCLA), I took classes with one of the swim instructors. She boasted that she had never failed at teaching anyone how to swim. I proved her wrong!

I was in Guatemala for a summer many years ago during medical school. One of the other students I met there was a daughter of a Navy SEAL. She also mentioned how great of a swim coach she was. She declared she would make a swim convert out of me.

I proved her wrong too.

After proving so many people wrong, I came to believe I was simply one of those people who simply can't swim and I was destined to observe the water from the shore. I would live into my old age not experiencing some of the water activities that my soul had been waiting to meet.

To be quite honest, I have not let my lack of swimming capabilities completely stop me from enjoying water and some supervised water activities like snorkeling. Who goes snorkeling when they cannot swim?

Recently, my kids started taking consistent swim lessons. They were okay to begin with. But then, over the summer, they became great. They started competing with other swim teams. After the summer swim season, the team gave awards. Of the approximately seventy kids on the swim team, they chose three people for awards. My two girls got two of the three awards. Not because they were the best swimmers but because they were the most *improved* swimmers. Their coach once said that watching them swim moved her to tears. So they've come a long way.

We went to the ocean recently, and for the second time, my daughter said, "Mommy, I want to learn how to surf." Here I was, thinking to myself, "Are my kids gonna be in the water surfing while I stay at the shore watching them, praying they don't need my help?" That became the reason I decided I had to try again.

I reenrolled for a swimming class. This time felt urgent because I already know my kids are going to be doing more crazy stuff in water.

On my very first day, the swim coach asked what I could do in the water. She asked, "Can you put your face in water?" I said, "Yes, I can." So I put my face in the water. She said, "Okay, good. We can do some stuff." And then she said, "Okay, let me see what you have. Let's see you swim across the pool."

And for the first time in my life, I actually used the coaching tools I've acquired over the last couple of years, similar to how I teach the women to master their money. I employed a similar mentality, but this time, it was for swimming.

I swam across the whole pool successfully. Yeah! And within this thirty-minute class, I was able to learn how to turn on my back so I could breathe. While waiting for the teacher to teach another student, I decided to just see if I could even float using the mindset tools I'd learned. And for the first time in my life, I started floating in water.

I realized that what helped me the most was understanding and believing that swimming can be simple and easy. If it wasn't simple, how come so many humans (including children) could do it? If *they* can, then I must be missing some simplicity in it. And so I told myself, "Swimming is simple. Swimming is easy." And that thought was why I was able to float. I was willing to go through the discomfort of water in my nose. I knew I wasn't going to die. They were not going to let me!

I've taken classes from better, more trained, more distinguished instructors. But until I told myself that I could succeed, I didn't. I had to unlearn the story that I told myself, that no one could teach me to swim.

My point is, those same tools that I teach women for money are the same tools that I used to learn how to swim and float for the first time. Those teaching tools are the things that have been missing. It's not that I was a bad swimmer. I just needed some practical tools and the power of my mindset. So if you think you are bad with money, it's not because you are bad with money. Rather, you may be missing the simplicity of money. You've also just never been taught the tools or incorporated it in a way that made sense for you.

Building a million-dollar and beyond net worth requires a wealthy-mind rewiring. Choosing to live well and richly requires a mindset change. You have to change the foundation because otherwise, your money house will be built on shaky grounds. We all know what happens when that occurs.

There are many ways to build and most require FOMO, hustle, overworking, grinding, and building wealth in a way that is not healthy.

In order to do it differently, we have to unlearn.

In order to do it differently, we have to learn differently.

As women physicians, we are at the highest risk of burnout. We earn less on average. However, in order to live life on our terms, we have to be willing to be different, live differently, and think differently. We can't do the same thing and expect a different result.

As researchers, we know the importance of hypothesis, experiments, observing results, and then tweaking the experiments in order to create a different result.

It's time to extend that into our money life.

We will no longer wait and be victims of a world built on a foundation of oppressive systems and social conditioning within and outside of medicine that was not made with us in mind. We are learning, reframing, and changing our money mentality, patterns, actions, and stories.

We are taking our money into our own hands, and that is a great thing.

Money is a tool for freedom, a tool for change, and a tool for good.

I can't think of more worthy hands.

This is the only way to do it "right." When we take the time to learn this, we pour gasoline on our net worth. We grow that net worth in a way that is accelerated without burning out in the grind.

I imagine a world where physicians being good with money is the norm. Having a six-, seven-figure net worth is just the way things are. No big deal. A world where women physicians are paid proportionally to the value we bring. A world where wealth disparities no longer exist due to our gender and race. A world where physicians are leading again.

No one is coming to fix this for us, and that's a great thing. Because if they come, they can leave at will. We are fixing it ourselves. We are women physicians. We lead. We are leading well, richly, and fully without sacrificing our well-being. We are redefining money and wealth in a way that benefits all of us, not just a select few.

The doors to wealth are jammed open. You get to choose.

This is a money revolution. Are you coming?

I founded The MoneyFitMD Money School for badass women physicians as the answer to this change. An exclusive coaching community for women physicians who want to grow their net worth to the six or seven figures and beyond without the drama of money past. You learn the coaching tools to manage your money brain, the highest yield financial education suited for busy physicians. Growth happens solo, but exponential growth happens in communities. The financial tools you learn will liberate you, elevate you, and place you in a financial space of freedom that you deserve to luxuriate in. This education bridges the gap our medical training left agape with regard to money. You get the accountability and the richness of a growing community of other badass women physicians who are committed to empowering each other and normalizing conversations around money.

We are redefining what it means to be women in medicine.

We are showing the world what wealth should look like: diverse and badass, just like you.

When you grow your wealthy mindset, your wealth grows. The math becomes the simple part. Every day in this community, we are celebrating women who are taking their power back, curating their own rich life.

We are a diverse group, and we believe that money in the hands of women physicians is key to changing medicine. We believe that closing wealth gaps among physicians starts with us.

I hope you will join us. Checkout www.moneyfitmd.com/msb to join us as we change the future of money for women physicians.

It's your time.

Thank you for allowing me to spend this time with you. Doing this work has been one of the biggest honors of my life.

Acknowledgments

Thank you to God, without whom the idea of this book would never have happened.

Thank you to all the women physicians who continue to show me that everything is possible.

We simply have to start with a belief!

Finally, thank you to my husband and our family. You keep inspiring me to be bigger and act on my dreams.

Made in the USA
Coppell, TX
14 July 2023